With all kind wishes.

Bewerunce?

14. 9. 53

FOUR ESSAYS IN
ACCOUNTING
THEORY

FOUR ESSAYS IN

ACCOUNTING THEORY

BY

F. SEWELL BRAY

F.C.A., F.S.A.A.

STAMP-MARTIN PROFESSOR OF ACCOUNTING

Published for
The Incorporated Accountants' Research Committee
by
GEOFFREY CUMBERLEGE
OXFORD UNIVERSITY PRESS
LONDON NEW YORK TORONTO
1953

Oxford University Press, Amen House, London E.C.4

GLASGOW NEW YORK TORONTO MELBOURNE WELLINGTON
BOMBAY CALCUTTA MADRAS KARACHI CAPE TOWN IBADAN

Geoffrey Cumberlege, Publisher to the University

PRINTED IN GREAT BRITAIN

TO
ACCOUNTANTS
EVERYWHERE

FOREWORD

I AM indeed honoured to write a foreword to these four essays by Professor Bray. They are the substance of addresses given by him on different occasions during the past year or so. As usual, they are distinguished by Professor Bray's challenging approach to any facet of accounting technique. I can think of no better tonic for an accountant than to read these essays. That they will be a tonic and a refreshment to those who read them is the sincere wish of his colleague and friend.

C. PERCY BARROWCLIFF
President of the Society of
Incorporated Accountants

CONTENTS

PREFACE

I HAVE been persuaded to bring together four research lectures which I gave at one place or another, mostly during the academic year 1951-2. They are set forth here as they were prepared, and as a consequence there are some overlappings which I hope may be treated as interconnecting links. No doubt the theme is much the same everywhere. Nevertheless, they embody a sincere attempt to cast around for such ideas as might push forward and develop the subject of accounting. I believe in accounting, and I want it to hold its own with other intellectual disciplines.

I felt I must also include as an appendix the preliminary report on *The Measurement of Productive Efficiency* prepared by a sub-committee of the Incorporated Accountants' Research Committee in the spring of 1951. I have made good use of it myself, and I frequently turn back to it for help and guidance.

I extend to the authors and publishers of all works from which quotations have been taken my thanks for their co-operation in granting permission to quote extracts from their publications. I am also grateful to the editors of the *Journal of the Social and Statistical Inquiry Society of Ireland* for permission to reproduce the paper on *Company Accounting*, to the editor of the *Incorporated Statistician* for permission to reproduce the paper on *Accounting and Statistical Relationships*, and to the editors of *Accounting Research* and the Cambridge University Press for permission to reproduce the articles on *Accounting Principles* and *The Measurement of Productive Efficiency*.

All four lectures were prepared in the Department of Applied Economics at Cambridge, and the Director has kindly given permission for their publication in the present form by the Incorporated Accountants' Research Committee.

1952

I

ACCOUNTING PRINCIPLES

The substance of an address given on
15 September 1951
at a course for
Incorporated Accountants
in Caius College, Cambridge

ACCOUNTING PRINCIPLES

'Those who are wont to judge by feeling are blind to
methods of reasoning, for they want to see at a glance,
and are not accustomed to seek out principles. And
others, contrariwise, who are wont to argue by principles, are blind to matters of feeling, for they look for
principles and cannot see at a glance.'

PASCAL[1]

1. The rules of an acquired skill, when brought to the settled
tendency of habit and committed to textbooks, are very apt to
be mistaken for fundamental doctrines when they are still little
more than the discrete boundaries of an empirically constructed
technique.

2. We are all of us products of our training and environment,
and the subject of accounting principles when brought into one
of our Cambridge courses ought to be managed as a refresher talk
on settled practices. So I thought and so I intended, but when I
came to revise the appropriate professional writings as a means of
preparation for this address, I was startled to find that I enter-
tained doubts about some established methods which I had always
taken for principles. Instead of dogmatizing, therefore, as I should,
I would like to spend time on re-examining some of our precon-
ceptions, and perhaps some of our predilections.

3. I prefer to think of a principle as a fundamental concept and
not as a rule to guide conduct, because I believe that as applied to
accounting this will give it tenets which in the long run will secure
its status. Rules, practices, conventions, and procedures may
change, but principles ought to prevail.

4. Many of our so-called accounting principles are little more
than working rules of practice, and some outsiders have called us
'pattern-followers', a description with a lurking criticism. Canning,
writing in 1929, remarked that 'It is still too early to give the name
of "principles" to more than a few elements of accountancy. It is

---

[1] Dr. H. F. Stewart's translation (Routledge & Kegan Paul, 1950, p. 11, para.
21).

misleading, to say the least, to attach that name to statistical procedures that, on their face, are compromise measures. "Working rules" more aptly describe the great bulk of procedure.[1] In 1951 I still find myself in substantial agreement with those remarks, but this should come as no surprise. Accountants have a preponderating concern with enterprises, and an enterprise 'is a creation of men capable of many changes at their will and capable of use by successors to its organisers.'[2]

5. If we go to the root of the matter I think we can detect two sources from which all *accounting* principles should spring; the first is conceptual, the second is natural. I take them in turn.

6. First, there are two general economic concepts which are quite central and fundamental to the practice of accounting. I refer to the concept of periodic income and the concept of wealth. You and I are the practical measurers of both, and I am quite sure that I do not need to remind you of the advantages to be associated with a measure of income which is stable in both form and content.

7. Second, all transactions which we usually record and epitomize are by nature either real or financial, actual between two entities or imputed in the accounts of one entity. Perhaps it will be clearer if I add that a *real* transaction is a money measurement of goods and services, and that provision for depreciation is an example or type of imputed transaction.

8. I sometimes think it is wise to look at what we are accounting for against the general background of economic history not long past, and I would like to temporarily arrest our discussion to sketch it. The reasons for so doing will show themselves later.

9. You will remember that financial disturbances assumed importance in the latter half of the nineteenth century, and eventually much was done to prevent people losing money, without knowing it, by investment in undesirable ventures. I suggest that much of our company legislation owes its origin to these incidents in our economic life, and that from them we ultimately derive the notion of *money* capital preservation.

---

[1] *The Economics of Accountancy, a Critical Analysis of Accounting Theory*, by J. B. Canning (The Ronald Press Co., New York, 1929).

[2] Op. cit., p. 234.

10. The First World War brought in its trail serious money troubles, and much thought was given to policies which aimed at stabilizing purchasing power. In the result deflationary influences were provoked and the economy had to meet a persistent problem of unemployment. Fiscal policies of full employment were sought, and, largely because of the circumstances of a second war, they have been virtually achieved. And yet, despite conditions of full employment, we again face price level instability and the added problems of productive efficiency. Plainly there are a number of variables in the system which we should like to hold constant at a high level of activity.

11. Difficulties of the sort which seriously affect prices force into question empirically devised measures of income. There in a nutshell is the immediate historical background which should drive us to look for the enduring principles in our theories.

12. Modern textbook versions of accounting theory tend to base themselves upon a set of conventions and doctrines.[1] By conventions they usually mean customs, and by doctrines rules of procedure. I think there are one or two principles to be found in both camps, but in any case I should prefer a re-sorting which recognized the distinction between principles and practices. It seems to me the principles are few; perhaps, at most, five in number.

13. First, the familiar idea of double-entry is quite fundamental to all accounting theory, however we care to explain it. I am told that the Russians have a system of triple-entry, although what this can mean I cannot yet imagine. I suspect that its roots must still lie in the ancient *principle* of double-entry, for elementally it seems quite axiomatic that if there is a receiver of money or its equivalent, then there must also be a payer, and, as we well know, money is the normal standard for measuring the exchange of goods and services.

14. Second, we cannot begin to shape accounts until we have conceived either the unit of organized activity, or the transactor whose history and condition we wish to measure and portray in financial terms. Plainly we must look at the transactions which take place under one roof, whatever that roof may be. I therefore regard

---

[1] Cf. *Advanced Accounting*, by Yorston, Smyth, and Brown (Australia, The Law Book Co. of Australasia Pty. Ltd., 1949).

the entity notion of accounting theory as primary. If you keep to the provisos I am about to mention you can make the entity what you will. It may be a firm, a person, or a company; it may be legal or domestic, a group or an isolationist; it may ascend or descend the hierarchy of economies to be limited at will by political, geographical, industrial, or natural boundaries; but whatever province we do choose to account for we know that it must have a real existence, and it must be significant for the purposes which finally resolve the structure of all accounts. I refer to the measurement of periodic income and the measurement of wealth.

15. Third, when enterprise is involved, accounting based on the measurement of periodic income looks at its responsibilities from the standpoint of *continuing* entities. I dignify the continuing entity concept as a principle. To my way of thinking it is one of the most fundamental of accounting principles because it implies the maintenance of all such facilities as will secure the operating[1] existence of an entity: equally this implies the maintenance of an ability to earn income as well as keep itself in being. You will at once see that a principle which orders adjuncts to a power of survival goes right to the core of economic stability. I concede that some of the technically engrained practices born of this principle may be open to question; but surely, however we may stray in interpreting it, there can be no doubts about the principle itself.

16. Fourth, if accounting measurements are to be objectively reliable, then accounting methods must be *consistently* employed. As you and I understand it, accounting should be a complete, *consistent*, and logical system. There should be no room for anything that is unnecessarily arbitrary. I therefore regard *consistency* as a principle because it safeguards accounting measurements from both the errors of whim and fancy and premeditated misrepresentation. You will readily see, however, that much care and attention must be given to the choice of methods which exemplify this principle if we are to penetrate through to its universal sanction in times of qualitative and quantitative change.

17. Fifth, I said earlier that, as it seemed to me, the two general economic concepts of periodic income and of wealth were central

[1] Or functional.

and fundamental to the practice of accounting. Income, as we all know, is devoted to consumption expenditure and saving, while at bottom wealth implies a store of *real* assets. As I have tried to show elsewhere[1] it should not be difficult to see that income is equal to consumption expenditure[2] plus saving, and that fundamentally saving is resolved in asset formating (or if you so prefer, capital) expenditure which constitutes an addition to wealth. I think this gives rise to a formal principle of accounting design which is expressed by a set of fundamentally related accounts: one, to measure periodic income; two, to show its transfer[3] and disposition; three, to explain the application of retained income or saving, its effect upon wealth, and capital changes, and, four, to measure and portray those resources which together make up the wealth of an entity. If I choose to rely on the terminology of accounting usage and relate it to a business enterprise, you will recognize a profit and loss account, an appropriation account, a capital reconciliation statement,[4] and a balance-sheet.[5]

18. And now let us have a look at some of the technical practices to which accounting principles give rise. So far as we in this country are concerned the most authoritative statement has come from the Council of the Institute of Chartered Accountants in England and Wales. While, in retrospect, I tend to think the title of accounting principles assumed in that statement was a misnomer, the preamble made it clear that what it really contained was recommendations to members of the Institute on *certain aspects* of the *accounts of companies*. In addition to this double

---

[1] *The Accounting Mission* (Melbourne University Press for The Commonwealth Institute of Accountants, 1951; Great Britain: Cambridge University Press).

[2] Although the consumption expenditure of one period is not necessarily motivated by the income of the same period.

[3] Coming and going.

[4] Cf. *Some Accounting Terms and Concepts*, A Report of a Joint Exploratory Committee appointed by The Institute of Chartered Accountants in England and Wales and by The National Institute of Economic and Social Research (Cambridge University Press, 1951).

[5] As will be noted in *The Accounting Mission*, I prefer the descriptions (i) Operating or Activity, (ii) Income and Outlay, (iii) Resting, and (iv) Capital or Balance Sheet, for the economic reasons there assigned to them.

limitation there was a clear emphasis on practice, as the following quotation shows: 'Whilst it is recognized that the form in which accounts are submitted to shareholders is (subject to compliance with the Companies Act) a matter within the discretion of directors, it is hoped that these recommendations will be helpful to members in advising, in appropriate cases, as to what is regarded as the best practice.' I think we must all be grateful to the Council of the Institute for the immediate practical help which they gave to us, particularly in regard to those questions where in the existing circumstances practising uniformity was plainly desirable.

19. I do not think you would wish me to recite or comment upon that detailed statement of practices; many of them have now passed into the Companies Act of 1948, and I know they are more than familiar to you all. If you will allow, I should prefer to concentrate upon such subsequent developments as seem to me to come a little closer to the inner meaning of some of those originating principles I set out in the first part of this paper. We all agree on the necessity for order and method in the preparation and presentation of accounts,[1] the need for adequate disclosure of exceptional and essential items, the validity of consistent methods of valuation, and, if monetary measurement distortion seems to have been but lightly touched upon, at least the poser has been plainly indicated.

20. If you will look back at the general tenor of what I have called accounting principles I think you will sense a dichotomy between the real and the financial. There can be no gainsaying the practical problems which have latterly come forward, and which are directly traceable to this source. I have only to instance two quotations taken from the City Notes, in *The Times* of 25 May 1951. First:

Doubtless the question of the amount and form of information which directors should give to shareholders may never be solved to everybody's satisfaction. Sometimes there seems to be almost a sense of conflict between the strict duty of giving audited accounts of stewardship and the wider aim of giving information that is not so much an account of the past as an effort to enable shareholders to judge the present fortunes and future prospects of their property.

[1] Cf. *Design of Accounts* (3rd ed., Oxford University Press, 1949).

Second:

The conception of accounts as the record of the board's trusteeship and the expenditure of the proprietor's funds, with its allied conception of the auditors as the shareholders' watchdogs, points to the historical method. But the conception of accounts as a vehicle of maximum useful information to shareholders on the general position and prospects of their company may point to replacement values. Ideally company accounts must recognize both these conceptions and serve both purposes. But it is arguable that revaluation is in any case something which can only happen once in a way, after a major period of sustained inflation, and that it need not really conflict with or impair the more elementary and indispensable record of what has happened to the money.

21. Depreciation practices in the light of the dichotomy between the real and the financial are receiving a sufficient airing all round just now; what I want to fasten on to here are the questions of formal presentation and the treatment of inventories which it also raises.

22. Balance-sheet items, in accordance with present practice, are more or less grouped under such headings as fixed assets, interests in subsidiaries and associated companies, current assets, capital and reserves, debentures and long-term liabilities, current liabilities, and provisions. Other headings may be required to comply with statute or according to taste, but this simple enumeration will suffice to give the general picture. We sometimes find a category of investments included under fixed assets, and almost without exception stocks of raw materials and finished goods, and inventories of work in progress or process, take pride of place under current assets. I confess that I have never quite understood what was meant by the qualification 'fixed' as applied to assets; moreover, I have never quite touched bottom on the fundamental distinction between fixed and current assets. Nevertheless, the Institute's statement does help us by implication, for we are told that: 'Fixed assets, whatever be their nature or the type of business in which they are employed, have the fundamental characteristic that they are held with the object of earning revenue and not for the purpose of sale in the ordinary course of business.'[1] Current

---

[1] IX. 'Depreciation of Fixed Assets', January 1945, Gee & Co. (Publishers), Ltd., London.

assets include 'such assets as are held for realisation in the ordinary course of business'.[1] These quotations imply that the distinction between fixed and current is found by applying the test of realization in the ordinary course of business.

23. I wonder, however, if this *is* such a fundamental grouping test as it appears to be, more particularly if we cease to limit the accounting entity to the business enterprise. I would also like to draw your attention to a significant sub-grouping of fixed assets which has recently made its appearance in the balance-sheet of Imperial Chemical Industries Ltd. I refer to the clear distinction there made between *physical* assets and intangible assets. I welcome this development because it emphasizes the category of the physical and the *real*.

24. A balance-sheet is the accounting means of employing certain valuation conventions to measure entity wealth, capital and reserves, net worth, or whatever expression you choose to select for what is nothing more than a measure of capital in the general sense of that term. The fundamental purpose of a balance-sheet, therefore, is to measure capital and to show its set up in the form of integral aggregates of assets and liabilities. Whilst it is important to indicate ownership claims on capital, they are secondary to its primary measurement.

25. Now, I want to suggest to you that if we fall back on the principles which are formal, and on those which connote the entity, continuity, and consistency, and apply them to the balance-sheet façade, then we must bump up against a cardinal distinction between *real* and financial aggregates. It is implicit in all quasi balance-sheet consolidations and quite plain in closed and complete ones.

26. In a recent article, prepared to explain a national balance-sheet, I wrote:

Accountants usually denote the money valuation contents of a balance sheet in terms of what they are accustomed to regard as the fundamental equation of accounts. It is simply expressed thus—Assets minus Liabilities equals Capital. We should wish to expand this equation to read—

[1] VIII. 'Form of Balance Sheet and Profit and Loss Account' July 1944, Gee & Co. (Publishers), Ltd.

Real Assets plus Asset Claims minus Liability Claims equals Capital. In our view this description points to a fundamental classification informing the structure of all balance sheets. It emphasises the pivotal significance of monetary claims for the process of consolidation, and it isolates a measure of *real* wealth. Asset and liability claims may be brought, conveniently and concisely, within the categories long term, short term, and deferred. Real assets will ordinarily comprise the fixed assets of accounting terminology and inventories.[1]

For the moment we will leave on one side the problem of inventories and deal with the balance-sheet grouping for fixed assets. Despite its ambiguity I am disinclined to change a description which by now is so engrained in practice. In any case, apart from inventories, we all agree that it should contain the accounting valuation of *real* assets. Accordingly, I should take in the method of Imperial Chemical Industries, and impose on the fixed asset grouping a limitation denoted by the following inset or subheadings.

1. *Real* or physical.
2. Deferred expenditure benefiting the activities of future accounting periods.
3. Intangible.

Again, apart from inventories, *all* other balance-sheet aggregates are virtually financial or money claims, and, as I note above, these can be conveniently and concisely categorized as long-term, short-term, and deferred. Whatever additional disclosure explanations may be required, either by statute or otherwise, I have a preference for such descriptions of claims, whether asset or liability; they seem to me simple, clear, and universal.

27. And now let us have a look at the problem of inventories. I first want to explain in the simplest possible terms what is meant by the economic use of the expression inventory profit or loss, and for this purpose I will engage in some abstractions. Assume an enterprise which begins and ends its accounting period with identical quantities of identical stocks. Assume that the bases of valuation are those of more or less traditional accounting practice

---

[1] *Accounting Research*, vol. ii, No. 3, July 1951, p. 281.

(that is, first cost or lower market-value), that stocks are frequently and regularly turned over in their entirety, and that the enterprise has encountered substantial short-period increases in the buying prices of its stocks. In these circumstances, it should be clear to all of us that the carrying value of the closing stocks will be greater than the carrying value of the opening stocks, despite the fact that they are identical in quantity and kind. This means that the difference between the two valuations will form part of the accounting measure of profit. It is this part which is called inventory profit. I leave it to you to work out for yourselves what is meant by inventory loss. Now although my assumptions may seem unreal they are not *so* far distant from that situation in which by far the greater part of a company's investment in inventories is virtually a fixed asset because it is essential to the *continuation* of the company's operations at an effective level of output. You will recognize that this situation is *not* uncommon.

28. I am myself convinced that inventory profits and losses are substantial in periods beset by noticeable price changes, and this circumstance is peculiarly relevant to those enterprises which *have to carry* heavy inventories. If selling margins happen to be low we can easily see what a disconcerting and distorting influence is brought to bear on the accounting measurement of operating income. Moreover, as some writers never tire of telling us, an element of inventory profit is itself represented in the closing inventory valuation. Plainly this is not yet a realized profit available for *immediate* distribution; nevertheless, it will almost certainly involve an increased tax liability.

29. I am inclined to think the time has come for the application of more rational practices to the measurement of profit, in the circumstances I have indicated. You will recognize that accounting measures of periodic income have social consequences. For example, they have some influence on those questions which concern the distribution and redistribution of income, under whatever guise they are presented. In *our* textbooks it is the dividend distributions of corporate enterprise or the claims of the Inland Revenue, but these are by no means all.

30. And so I arrive at the following conclusions. In so far as the

major portion of the inventory of an enterprise *does* constitute a fixed asset necessary to the *continuation* of effective operations, it is my view that it should be classified as such in the balance-sheet. In this case it also seems to me that inventory profits or losses should be excluded from the measurement of operating income, but I add the proviso, perhaps only very exceptionally required, that a loss must be recovered by appropriation out of either previously accumulated price-change profits (the usual means), or current income, where not to do so would do anything to impair the protection of contributed money-capital implied by legal sanction. I also wish to make clear my view that where inventories can be liquidated without doing hurt to the long-run stability and operating activity of an enterprise, then there is little need to bother with inventory profits or losses, for then the inventories themselves are little more than speculative asset claims. The essence of the inventory problem resides in the fundamental distinction between fixed and speculative holdings.

31. The measurement of current inventory costs does not present great difficulties, and there is a clear case for *pegging* opening and closing valuations in those cases where the physical content constitutes a *continuing* investment necessary to activity. Surely no one can urge that accounting practices should countenance the inclusion of unrealized windfall gains within a customary measurement of operating income.

32. I add one further comment. A change in the design of plant output may bring additional inventories into the continuing investment category. These additions should be financed either out of savings or borrowings, because they constitute *real* asset formation. If for any reason this revised level of inventory investment is drawn upon without any conscious change in the scale of output, then provision must be made to cover its replacement in conditions of rising current costs[1] if continuity is to be financially safeguarded.

33. I should like to close this address with one last general observation. The process of measuring periodic income and wealth accumulation is essentially an accounting procedure, but we cannot abstract from accounts interpretations which rest upon philo-

---

[1] Equivalent to current cost less liquidated carrying cost.

sophical issues incapable of expression in accounting terms. If time had allowed, I should have wished to explore the relevance of mathematical principles to expectation accounting. I believe there is some evidence for supposing that the formal structure of accounts can be shown to more or less depend upon the magnitude of a few significant variables, but this inquiry must be held over for a later occasion.

2

COMPANY ACCOUNTING

The substance of a paper given to the
Statistical and Social Inquiry Society of Ireland
in the Royal Irish Academy
on 23 May 1952

COMPANY ACCOUNTING

1. I suspect that some of you will think it a trifle odd that I should seek to impose upon a learned society a dissertation on company accounting, and perhaps I should clear my conscience by confessing to some doubts when I first came to seriously contemplate its preparation. Now that I have worked through to the end of my thesis I firmly believe that no one should question the importance of the subject-matter. Company accounts which disclose clear reports of stewardship have beneficial social implications. Company accounts designed as constitutional portrayals of income generation and wealth accumulation are sources of vital statistical information about economic activity over a large part of the enterprise sector of a national economy.

2. I understand that just at present the legal sanctions with accounting status touching companies in your country are still very largely to be found in the Companies (Consolidation) Act of 1908. In my part of the world, as you know, we have twice amended this piece of legislation. First, we had the Companies Act of 1929, and now we have the comparatively recent Act of 1948. To those of us who have been brought up under the shadows of the Acts of 1929 and 1948, the accounting standards of the 1908 Act look both meagre and sparse. Section 26 of that Act makes mention of the contents of a balance-sheet in the broadest terms. It requires that the summary accompanying the annual list of members must (except where the company is a private company) include a statement 'in the form of a balance sheet, audited by the Company's auditors, and containing a summary of its share capital, its liabilities, and its assets, giving such particulars as will disclose the general nature of those liabilities and assets, and how the values of the fixed assets have been arrived at', but it is also made quite plain that the balance-sheet need not include a statement of profit and loss. It seems to me that we cannot but regard the absence of some form of periodic profit and loss measure as a blemish, for without it there is little to aid the understanding of those responsible members of society who need to assess a company's operating

effectiveness. You will also notice the disclosure exemption conferred upon private companies in the reference I have cited. This tends to veil the financial position of constitutionally secluded companies. These companies may, in fact, engage in very considerable activities, of importance both for the well-being of the nation and those who have had the ability and foresight to start and keep them going. An adequate disclosure of financial information engenders confidence over a wide area, and providing there is no risk to the exercise of reasonable freedom and enterprise, I believe it makes for the vigorous continuance and development of corporate activities.

3. I recognize there has always been a weight of opinion favourable to exemption privileges for private companies. This is readily understandable if we look at the small family business to be found at one end of the scale of private company activities. The goodwill of the business is a personal one and there is a natural inclination to preserve it within the family. At the other end of the scale is the private company which is nothing more than a subsidiary of a public company, and in some cases it is a wholly owned subsidiary. It is clear that in pliable hands the subsidiary private company device could be used to minimize the disclosure of group information to the public. It could also be used to lay off a highly speculative venture. In between both ends of the scale are a number of private companies conducting quite sizeable enterprises, with or without other non-controlling companies as shareholders.

4. I believe that limited liability is still a privilege. All privileges imply duties, and in this case intelligible accounting disclosure is surely the obligation of the privilege. It cannot be doubted that grantors of trade credit ought to have an adequate means of financial information; both creditors and shareholders have a direct interest in company accounting disclosure. Less directly, but still I think sagaciously, those promoters of the public interest who are concerned with the continuation and expansion of effective enterprise as a means of securing economic development should be able to inform their judgements by reference to published accounts. In the long run there is little to be lost but much to be gained by

revealing the economic status of those corporate entities which substantially contribute to the wants and add to the wealth of a progressive nation.

5. I think there can be little doubt that one of the serious defects in the 1908 Act was the lack of recognition of the *domestic* entity constituted by a holding company and its subsidiary companies. In that Act the concept of *legal* entity was paramount. If I may, I should like at this point to draw on an address which I recently gave to an accountants' course at Cambridge. I was there examining the nature of accounting principles and during the course of my discussion I said that

we cannot begin to shape accounts until we have conceived either the unit of organized activity, or the transactor whose history and condition we wish to measure and portray in financial terms. Plainly we must look at the transactions which take place under one roof, whatever that roof may be. I therefore regard the entity notion of accounting theory as primary. If you keep to the provisos I am about to mention you can make the entity what you will. It may be a firm, a person, or a company; it may be legal or domestic, a group or an isolationist; it may ascend or descend the hierarchy of economies to be limited at will by political, geographical, industrial, or natural boundaries; but whatever province we do choose to account for we know that it must have a real existence, and it must be significant for the purposes which finally resolve the structure of all accounts. I refer to the measurement of periodic income and the measurement of wealth.[1]

6. Whilst no one would question the superior necessity for accounts of legal entities, especially where creditor claims are important, the domestic outlook of a holding company and its substratum companies is very similar to that of one company operating a number of branches. The several activities are centrally organized, and policy depends upon control. In such circumstances it cannot be denied that group measures of income and wealth are both significant and informative.

7. Where a group of companies is conducted as one economic entity by one management, the members of the legal parent should

[1] *Accounting Principles.* An address given on 15 Sept. 1951 at a course for Incorporated Accountants in Caius College, Cambridge.

have some means of judging the financial strength and income-earning ability of the group. Intelligent members of the parent company, and interested spectators of the group's affairs, will require more information on underlying undertakings than is commonly to be found in a balance-sheet item described as 'investments in subsidiary companies'. An adequate view of a group situation requires, at the very least, some assessment of the aggregate make-up of operating assets and monetary claims.

8. The technical details of company accounting consolidations are well known to accountants and do not require precise treatment here. What does need emphasis is the requirement of uniformity. A really meaningful system of aggregates can only be achieved if the underlying details are set up in forms dictated by uniform standards of clarity, sequence, order, and method. Both aggregation and consolidation presuppose accounting as a complete, consistent, and logical system of record and measure as related to a defined period of time. On the practical plane of accounting mechanics it was Mr. T. B. Robson who remarked that:

The preparation of consolidated accounts is greatly assisted by the adherence of all companies in the group to a uniform classification of accounting items and a standard accounting practice. The issue to all concerned of accounting instructions designed to secure conformity with this practice, not only as between companies but also as between one financial period and another, is of the greatest value. Many groups prepare monthly accounts on a consolidated basis, and the importance of having a clearly prescribed routine in such cases will be readily apparent.[1]

9. At this stage it is pertinent to remind you that one of the criticisms which had some part in prompting the new Companies Act in England was that reliable comment on and interpretation of published accounts was impeded by a lack of uniformity, and there is a sense in which it can now be said that the accounting provisions of the Companies Act, 1948, have established a minimum standard of uniformity in the presentation of company accounts. As we have also seen, there is an impelling constraint which requires us

[1] *Consolidated and Other Group Accounts*, by T. B. Robson, p. 37 (Gee & Co. (Publishers), Ltd., 2nd ed., 1950).

to put together component accounts in like form and content for a like period of time, if resultant consolidated accounts are to have any real significance. Consistency is, therefore, a matter of principle which applies as much to measurement as to form.

If accounting measurements are to be objectively reliable, then accounting methods must be consistently employed. There should be no room for anything that is unnecessarily arbitrary. Consistency safeguards accounting measurements from both the errors of whim and fancy, and from premeditated misrepresentation, but much care and attention must be given to the choice of methods which exemplify this principle if we are to penetrate through to its universal sanction in times of qualitative and quantitative change.[1]

I shall have more to say on this matter when we come to consider the valuation problems implicit in the presentation of accounts.

10. Although I have expressed an unhesitating preference for the presentation of consolidated accounts it must not be thought that there are *no* reservations. Thus, 'one company which is strong financially may be used as a cover for another company which is on the verge of insolvency'. Again, 'it frequently happens that large-scale undertakings are conducting different types of business, in which case any consolidation of accounts should be reasonably analysed to show the position of each type of industrial activity'.[2] Moreover, there are cases in which consolidation is impracticable, and although I do not wish to be led into an exhaustive treatment of these reservations, I should like to quote the following two paragraphs from Mr. T. B. Robson's book on *Consolidated and Other Group Accounts*.

It seems almost superfluous to say that group accounts need not deal with a subsidiary if the directors of the holding company are of opinion that this is impracticable. If the necessary information is not obtainable because, for example, a state of war or civil strife exists, or because there is no basis upon which the foreign currency assets, liabilities and earnings

---

[1] Cf. my address on *Accounting Principles* given on 15 Sept. 1951 at a course for Incorporated Accountants in Caius College, Cambridge.

[2] *Design of Accounts*, 3rd ed. by F. Sewell Bray and H. Basil Sheasby, pp. 8–9 (published for the Incorporated Accountants' Research Committee by Oxford University Press, 1949).

can be converted into the currency in which the group accounts are presented, clearly the group accounts could not deal with that information, and no legal obligation could alter this inescapable fact.

It is for the directors of the holding company to decide whether consolidation of any subsidiary's figures is practicable; they have, therefore, a reasonable business discretion in the matter. They should, however, bear in mind that the word 'impracticable', in the legal sense in which it is necessarily used in the Companies Act, has a meaning closely akin to 'impossible'. The word is not to be interpreted in the sense of 'troublesome' or 'inconvenient' in which it is often used loosely in conversation.[1]

Plainly there are some qualifications to the presentation of consolidated accounts when it comes to laying down statutory requirements.

11. Before I pass on to discuss the background of opinion which culminated in the British Act of 1948 I should like to remark, as a matter of history, on the surprising absence in the 1908 Act of any obligation to report in a prospectus on either the past profits or the net assets status of a company which invites the public to subscribe for its shares. I know it was once an old practice to state in a prospectus the average profits of a preceding range of years. Nevertheless, as my present audience especially will know, average figures can be very misleading and open to serious misinterpretation when projected into the realm of probability. Moreover, profits want defining, and I hold the view that any expectation based upon a past trend requires an explicit statement of the elements in the trend. The trend itself must be sufficiently long to be indicative of the immediate future, and consistency of measurement is quite fundamental. I should, therefore, expect to find these matters dealt with as statutory rules in any company legislation bearing upon the statement of profits in a prospectus. The need for a disclosure of net assets is obvious and can hardly require further explanation here.

12. The British Act of 1929 tidied up some of the deficiencies in the 1908 Act, but there were still gaps if the law was to be brought into line with the enlightened opinions of society. It was not

---

[1] Op. cit., p. 20.

surprising, therefore, when in June 1943 a committee was appointed 'to consider and report what major amendments are desirable in the Companies Act, 1929. . . .' This committee reported in June 1945.[1] It was satisfied by the evidence that the great majority of limited companies, both public and private, were honestly and conscientiously managed. It was also made clear that the system of limited liability companies had been and was 'beneficial to the trade and industry of the country and essential to the prosperity of the nation as a whole'. The committee considered 'that the fullest practicable disclosure of information concerning the activities of companies' would lessen opportunities for abuse 'and accord with a wakening social consciousness'. I regard this emphasis on disclosure as important, and I particularly ask you to mark the reference to a wakening social consciousness.

13. The introductory part of the Cohen Committee report gave a useful summary of those matters to which public attention had been drawn since the Act of 1929 came into force. These were dealt with under the headings of (a) Prospectuses, (b) Private companies, (c) Nominee shareholdings, (d) Accounts, and (e) Control. As company accounting is the subject of my talk, I hope you will bear with me if I quote in full what the committee said about accounts.

The present legal requirements as to the contents of the accounts to be presented to shareholders are too meagre. The practice of showing a number of diverse items in one lump sum, and thereby obscuring the real position as to the assets and liabilities and as to the results of trading, makes it difficult and often impossible for a shareholder to form a true view of the financial position and earnings of the company in which he is interested. While auditors have tended to press for standards in advance of the requirements of the present law, it has been suggested that their hands would be strengthened if the law were to accord more nearly with what they regard as the best practice.[2]

You will especially note that these observations applied to the accounting provisions of the Act of 1929, which were nothing like so slender as those of the Act of 1908.

---

[1] *Report of the Committee on Company Law Amendment* (London: H.M. Stationery Office, June 1945, Cmd. 6659).

[2] Op. cit., para. 7 (d), p. 8.

14. I know that you have been mercifully free from major financial scandals, and I suspect that questions of accounting disclosure to prevent abuse do not weigh heavily with you. Nevertheless, it is still my view that there is everything to be gained by producing accounts which give a clear and orderly picture of the activities of enterprise. Accurately designed and informative accounts make for greater effectiveness; they help those co-operating in economic activity to understand their own contributions to income generation; they assist economists and others to overcome those difficult social and economic problems which always press hard upon the heels of enterprise, and in a country which is developing manufacturing enterprise they should attract much-needed capital to efficiently run concerns. In the last resort increasing standards of living only result from increasing real product, and increasing real wealth accumulations made possible by saving part of that product. National aggregates of this order are but the sum totals of individual entity contributions, and whether that entity be a small farm or a major public company, those responsible for its management can only intelligently increase its level of productivity if they know with some accuracy what has so far been achieved. Expectations should be founded on clear and open accounts of the past. I agree that accounting cannot take the place of fertility in resource and imagination, but I do think that it can and does point out salient economic elements of strength and weakness. In this way it helps entrepreneurs to realize a 'capacity for imposing their authority on their organization and of persuading others to entrust them with the resources necessary for new ventures'.[1]

15. The Cohen Committee was interested in the financial implications of company accounts. The primary purpose of published company accounts is to convey adequate financial information in a form that can be assimilated by shareholders and creditors, and apart from a few inevitable tangles of accounting mechanics the British Act of 1948 has secured this end. Nevertheless, I feel that other purposes are slowly but inevitably coming into view. For example, the Cohen Committee considered suggestions framed

---

[1] Cf. Professor G. C. Allen's address to the British Association (*Economic Journal*, Sept. 1950).

with the object of relating accounts to general economic policy. Although I must confess to some disappointment at the line taken, I think it is instructive to look at what the committee said on this most forward-looking topic. I quote from the report:

We have also considered suggestions that, to assist those responsible for framing general economic policy, companies should be required to disclose in their accounts details of sales, expenses of production, selling and distribution, administration and management and other like details. In our view, however, such information could not be given in sufficient detail to achieve the object in view without loading the published accounts, of which the primary purpose is to convey financial information in a form that can be assimilated by shareholders and creditors, with so much detail as to fail in that purpose. We consider that information required for general economic purposes would be more appropriately and conveniently obtained through some such machinery as the Census of Production Act, under which information could be required in greater detail than would be practicable in published accounts.[1]

I do not myself feel that it is impossible to give information without overloading published company accounts. It is my view that a simple form of presentation can be devised which could be readily assimilated by shareholders and creditors, and set in a style which would also assist those responsible for framing general economic policy. As I said in my book on *The Measurement of Profit*: 'In the circumstances of the times it may well be that the machinery of the Census of Production Act is the better instrument to the fulfilment of national economic enquiries, but even such an instrument is not free from the immediate requirement of adaptation to the growing technique of Social Accounting.'[2]

16. I would now like to deal with the accounting material which seems to me to be appropriate to the requirements of an ideal Companies Act. I seek to outline a simple form of accounts which will meet all financial disclosure needs and at the same time make available useful and meaningful economic information. It is my own point of view that the two general economic concepts of periodic income and of wealth are central and quite fundamental to the

[1] *Report of the Committee on Company Law Amendment*, para. 97 (H.M. Stationery Office, June 1945).   [2] Oxford University Press, 1949, p. 46.

practice of accounting. Income, as most of us know, is devoted to consumption expenditure and saving, while at bottom wealth implies a store of real assets.

17. In a paper which I gave to the Australian Congress on Accounting at Sydney in November 1949 I dealt with the influence of economic ideas on the formal statement of accounts and the principles of accounting measurement. I drew attention to the fact that a substantial part of the subject-matter of economics is now brought under discussion and explained by reference to national aggregation of income and expenditure and their interrelation. I tried to explain in that paper that the problems which confronted economists in the applied field of income and expenditure studies necessitated certain empirical constructions and I put forward the claim that these constructions attained reliable proportions only when they were made to fit into the self-checking pattern of a double-entry system of accounts. I also suggested that this pattern must conform to certain primary economic concepts. As economists, and probably some accountants will know, these primary concepts in their simplest form are independently related in a closed economy in two ways. Thus, if we adopt the symbols—

$$I = \text{Income or Product}$$
$$C = \text{Consumption}$$
$$S = \text{Saving}$$
$$AF = \text{Asset Formation}$$
$$\text{then} \quad I = C + S$$
$$\text{and} \quad S = AF.$$

It will be recognized that these are the Keynesian identities of any accounting structure relevant to a nation's transactions. It is my view that these primary economic concepts as formally related give birth to a series of fundamental accounts which are just as relevant for firms or companies as for the nation as a whole. In fact, I would want to suggest that they are not only fundamental but universal as well, and that they constitute the key to all accounting designs. It should not be difficult to see that income is equal to consumption expenditure plus saving and that fundamentally saving is resolved in asset formating, or (as most accountants will prefer) capital, expenditure which constitutes addition to wealth. The series of related accounts, which taken together seem to me to constitute a formal principle of accounting design, may be expressed in the following manner: There should first be an account measuring periodic income; thereafter an account is required to show the transfer and disposition of that income; a third account is wanted to explain the application of retained income or saving, its effect upon wealth, and capital changes. A fourth and final form of accounting presentation is required to measure and portray those resources which together make up the wealth of an entity. Although accountants have been very largely placed at some distance from economic ideas, nevertheless they have come very near to using this type of structure. Thus, if I choose to rely on the terminology of accounting usage and relate it to a business enterprise, you will recognize a profit and loss account, an appropriation account, a capital reconciliation statement, and a balance-sheet. In a series of lectures which I gave to the Australian universities in 1949 I used the descriptions Operating or Activity, Income and Outlay, Resting, and Capital or Balance-sheet, but I did this for the economic reasons which I there assigned to them. Nevertheless, you will see that the formal pattern is much the same for whatever entity we choose to account for, whether it be a nation or a firm.

18. It is the function of a profit and loss account to assess the operating income of business activity. In America the same account is more commonly described as the Income Statement. In my opinion this is a title which should not be disregarded. In recent years both the profit and loss account and the income statement have undergone some modification. In England it is probable that some impetus was given to this development by the Kylsant case, which did much to draw attention to the desirability of disclosing the operating earnings of public companies. It also brought into prominence the unsatisfactory nature of undisclosed reserves. The Committee on Company Law Amendment specifically recommended that the profit and loss account should give a true and fair indication of the earnings or income of the period covered by the account, and that it should disclose any material respects in which it included extraneous or non-recurrent transactions or

transactions of an exceptional nature. This recommendation further provided 'that if in any such period a material change was made in the basis on which the account or any item therein was calculated, attention should be called to the change and to the effect thereof by way of a note on the account'.[1]

19. It seems to me that these recommendations are significant; they indicate a new trend in accounting thought, the general tenor of which is marked by a design which first lays emphasis on operating activity. Thus the operating section of the profit and loss account should draw attention to the result of the economic activity of an enterprise. As is well known, at the present stage of accounting technique this account is prepared in terms of a monetary dimension based on historical costs and historical revenues. For my part I should prefer a measure of operating profit or loss which did, in fact, encompass the effect of changes in the value of money in so far as these can be specifically related to adjustments for depreciation and the valuation of inventories, but I will comment rather more fully on these questions shortly. The operating section of a company's profit and loss account should be related to the main objects and purposes for which the company was constituted. Many companies are also engaged in other subsidiary activities which themselves yield profits or losses apart from the main activity. These subsidiary profits or losses should be calculated and portrayed by means of separate and subsidiary operating accounts. Thus the first part of the appropriation account ought to receive the main operating profit or loss of the company and be followed by the subsidiary profits or losses arising from its lesser activities. It should thereafter pick up the non-operating incomings and outgoings of the company on current account. These are entries very largely financial in character, as in the common example of a transfer income denoted by the entry 'dividends and interest on security investments'. In this way we should arrive at the total income of the company.

Thereafter we should also expect to find in the appropriation account these extraneous, non-recurrent, or exceptional items which are considered relevant to the results of the period. I feel that a

---

[1] *Report of the Committee on Company Law Amendment*, p. 61.

break should then be made in the appropriation account to show the manner in which the total income of the company (derived from all sources) is devoted to taxation and dividends, thereby resulting in a balance which is equivalent to the undistributed income or saving of the period. It might be well to make a further provision for the publication of such abnormal credits or charges as turn out to be related to previous periods and to show any withdrawals from reserve in the form of past accumulated savings covering current distributions. In one sense, however, such items are more appropriately dealt with in a capital reconciliation statement or, as I should prefer to call it, a resting account.

20. *Design of Accounts*, a Research Committee publication of the Society of Incorporated Accountants, which first appeared in 1944, recommended that 'published company revenue accounts should give a clear statement of operational profit, of non-operational items of income and expenditure, of provisions to meet liabilities defined as to time of accrual, of transfers to or from reserves clearly enunciated as such, and of the appropriation of residual balances'. In this book it was also suggested that every effort should be made to show the manner in which the true operating profit was built up, and the statement was made that 'accurately analysed revenue figures constitute a test of management, and in the case of published revenue accounts the share of each factor in production should be disclosed, as well as the net amount available for the owners'.

These developments have been partially given the force of statutory provision in the English Companies Act of 1948 with its requirements that 'every profit and loss account of a company shall give a true and fair view of the profit or loss of the company for the financial year';[1] and that

there shall be shown: (*a*) the amount charged to revenue by way of provision for depreciation, renewals or diminution in value of fixed assets; (*b*) the amount of the interest on the company's debentures and other fixed loans; (*c*) the amount of the charge for United Kingdom income tax and other United Kingdom taxation on profits, including, where practicable, as United Kingdom income tax any taxation imposed

[1] Section 149 (1).

elsewhere to the extent of the relief, if any, from United Kingdom income tax and distinguishing where practicable between income tax and other taxation; (*d*) the amounts respectively provided for redemption of share capital and for redemptions of loans; (*e*) the amount, if material, set aside or proposed to be set aside to, or withdrawn from, reserves; (*f*) . . . the amount, if material, set aside to provisions other than provisions for depreciation, renewals or diminution in value of assets or, as the case may be, the amount, if material, withdrawn from such provisions and not applied for the purposes thereof; (*g*) the amount of income from investments, distinguishing between trade investments and other investments; (*h*) the aggregate amount of the dividends paid and proposed.[1]

Moreover, the following matters are required to be stated by way of a note to the profit and loss account, if not otherwise shown:

(2) If depreciation or replacement of fixed assets is provided for by some method other than a depreciation charge or provision for renewals, or is not provided for, the method by which it is provided for or the fact that it is not provided for, as the case may be. (3) The basis on which the charge for United Kingdom income tax is computed. (4) Whether or not the amount stated for dividends paid and proposed is for dividends subject to deduction of income tax. (5) . . . the corresponding amounts for the immediately preceding financial year for all items shown in the profit and loss account. (6) Any material respects in which any items shown in the profit and loss account are affected:

(*a*) by transactions of a sort not usually undertaken by the company or otherwise by circumstances of an exceptional or non-recurrent nature; or

(*b*) by any change in the basis of accounting.[2]

We notice by way of comment that much emphasis is placed, and in our view rightly placed, on exposing to view a class of transaction which is related to the non-operating part of a company's income. It is good that there should be a growing social consciousness of the necessity for reasonable disclosure in the publication of company accounts. Nevertheless, as I commented in my book on *The Measurement of Profit*:

With such a marked stress on the one part of a company's current account in the interests of shareholding proprietors, it cannot but strike

---

[1] Eighth Schedule 12 (1).   [2] Eighth Schedule 14 (1) to (6).

the impartial observer as a little odd that no such requirements have been thought essential to cover the highly significant make-up of a company's operating account, more particularly when we come to regard the evident importance attached to the separate statement (aside from what should be its logical context) of 'amounts charged to revenue by way of provision for depreciation, renewals or diminution in value of fixed assets.' This wears an air of but half a story, and whatever the expedient arguments adduced to convince the legislature, presumably on the over-pressed score of protecting competing interests, we are sometimes tempted into feeling that at least one great opportune step to further the cause of such economic inquiries as are directed to the service of over-all financial stability has been lost by this failure to provide for a reasonable portrayal of the working account. Yet again, we may ask, what is the real objective significance attaching to the disclosure of an item of so-called profit which is, before charging or crediting a number of other operating and non-operating items, specifically required to be separately stated under the Act? By itself, whatever the purpose sought, such a figure is plainly ambiguous when judged from the standpoint of any acceptable accounting definition of operating surplus.[1]

21. It behoves us to look a little more closely into the operating section of a profit and loss account, for it is in this part of the account that we measure the real income derived from economic activity. Since it is real income in money terms that we are concerned with, we must first face the valuation problems implicit in its measurement. It will be known to most of you that accounting practices, as now applied to the periodic measurement of business income, were conceived in a time of relative price-level stability. I think it is no exaggeration to say that persistent depreciation in the value of money has called into question, with gathering momentum, the validity of some of these practices and has reached a point which compels their re-examination. The finance required to preserve operating assets so as to maintain production is a cause of anxiety to all who are concerned with the management and efficiency of industrial enterprises. Moreover, there is a serious danger of real capital consumption which accounting practices tend to veil.

22. Depreciation of real assets is an essential constituent of the input allocation for capital in any account of operating activity to

[1] Op. cit., p. 45.

measure business income. I do not think that company legislation, in attempting to define this account, should confine itself to questions of disclosure and form without touching upon the valuation of such an imputed item as depreciation. The conventional accounting view of depreciation has been described in terms of

that part of the cost of a fixed asset to its owner which is not recoverable when the asset is finally put out of use by him. Provision against this loss of capital is an integral cost of conducting the business during the effective commercial life of the asset and is not dependent upon the amount of profit earned. The assessment of depreciation involves the consideration of three factors: the cost of the asset, which is known; the probable value realisable on ultimate disposal, which can generally be estimated only within fairly wide limits; and the length of time during which the asset will be commercially useful to the undertaking. In most cases this last factor is not susceptible of precise calculation. Provisions for depreciation are, therefore, in most cases matters of estimation based upon the available experience and knowledge rather than of accurate determination. They require adjustment from time to time in the light of changes in experience and knowledge, including prolongation of useful life due to exceptional maintenance expenditure, curtailment due to excessive use, or obsolescence not allowed for in the original estimate of the commercially useful life of the asset.

Nothing could be clearer than this statement of depreciation accounting as commonly understood by professional accountants. It is quoted from the recommendations on accounting principles made by the Council of the Institute of Chartered Accountants in England and Wales: IX—Depreciation of Fixed Assets.[1]

23. This approach takes the general point of view that:

Fixed assets, whatever be their nature or the type of business in which they are employed, have the fundamental characteristic that they are held with the object of earning revenue and not for the purpose of sale in the ordinary course of business. The amount at which they are shown in the balance sheet does not purport to be their realisable value or their replacement value, but is normally an historical record of their cost less amounts provided in respect of depreciation, amortisation or depletion.[2]

As I have remarked elsewhere,[3] the accountant is necessarily

[1] January 1945, Gee & Co. (Publishers) Ltd., London.   [2] Op. cit.
[3] *The Measurement of Profit*, p. 67 (Oxford University Press, 1949).

concerned with the interests of proprietors, and by adopting this approach to depreciation he impliedly follows a course which looks both to the maintenance and stewardship of money capital expended on fixed assets, and the eventual recovery of all money costs out of revenues by way of the operating accounts. This practical solution, as I have already indicated, was developed during a period of relatively stable prices, and historically it is not difficult to show that it was bound up with a legal insistence on the stewardship of contributed money capital. As things have turned out it is doubtful whether this traditional accounting approach can now be supported. I am inclined to the view that we can still preserve by portrayal in company balance-sheets the stewardship of contributed money capital, while at the same time providing an adequate measure of *real* profit earned in company-operating accounts. The whole question takes on a different aspect as soon as we look beyond the money capital contributed by shareholders, and dividend distributions, to the means of safeguarding productive capacity by way of the maintenance of operating or activity assets; for then we begin to see our way through to a measurement of profit which does not disregard variations in *real* resources while concentrating upon variations in monetary claims.

24. For my part, I have never properly understood what was meant by the qualification 'fixed' as applied to assets. Apparently it has to be apprehended in conjunction with its sister qualification 'current', and the testing decision on whether or not assets are fixed or current is resolved by applying an accounting rule which answers the question whether or not assets are held for realization in the ordinary course of business. In the previous paragraph I quoted the statement of the Council of the Institute of Chartered Accountants in England and Wales that: 'Fixed assets, whatever be their nature or the type of business in which they are employed, have the fundamental characteristic that they are held with the object of earning revenue and not for the purpose of sale in the ordinary course of business.'[1] I add another statement of the same Institute to the effect that current assets include 'such assets as are

---

[1] *Recommendations on Accounting Principles*, IX—'Depreciation of Fixed Assets', January 1945, Gee & Co. (Publishers), Ltd., London.

held for realisation in the ordinary course of business'. I do not myself think that the asset grouping test of realization in the ordinary course of business is particularly fundamental. In my view entity wealth is made up of real assets and monetary claims, and the problems of accounting classification, as well as those of accounting measurement, appear in a new light as soon as we recognize the dichotomy between the real and the financial.

25. When we regard the matter from this standpoint we see that for a continuing entity it is the function of depreciation accounting to provide resources adequate to the replacement of *real* assets. Wear and tear by user, deterioration through time, and obsolescence take place quite independently of money values. Nevertheless, for the purposes of income measurement it is necessary periodically to attach some monetary value to these happenings. The orthodox accounting methods constitute a backward-looking view. They reach back to historical costs for their value assessments of current depreciation. The economic method is a more forward-looking approach, for the reason that it endeavours to measure depreciation by reference to current costs. No one can doubt, however, that the practical attempt to measure anticipated replacement costs of fixed operating assets within the period of their useful lives does present a number of awkward problems, although, as is always the case with comparatively new conceptions, some of the difficulties are over exaggerated. At periodical accounting dates, when the question of depreciation falls to be considered, the sensible approach would seem to require at least some reference to current replace-ment costs as better indicative of eventual replacement costs than original costs. This is particularly relevant in a period in which prices are steadily rising. Although it may be difficult to determine the current replacement cost of particular items of equipment, it should not prove impossible to arrive at a reasonable approxima-tion for main groups of fixed operating assets, if necessary by reference to statistical compilations of the periodical costs of capital goods.

26. I also think it well that it should not be overlooked in times of relatively temporary variations in prices, whichever way they go, that it is better to have regard to the general trend of replacement

costs rather than place too great a reliance on the last cost at the accounting date. Moreover, a situation will often arise in which an enterprise will not replace its worn-out equipment with something which is exactly the same. It may be more common to find that it will take on a new and possibly cheaper form of equipment contrived to fulfil similar functions more effectively. Much will depend upon the relevance of the immediate cost of the new asset to the original cost of the old asset, but in so far as the preservation of the money claims of the proprietors of the business is concerned, it seems clear to me that fixed asset cost recoveries by way of operating accounts should not fall below allocations based on the money expended as capital on the original asset. In this way we preserve the stewardship of contributed money capital.

In my book on *The Measurement of Profit* I have commented on the esoteric sense in which it is possible to urge that the purchasing power in real terms which was equivalent to the money cost of the original asset at the time of its acquisition should be stabilized, in which case the stewardship of contributed money capital is converted into a stewardship of real capital, and to comply with this view depreciation might be validly provided on the basis of the trend of general price levels at accounting dates.[1]

27. It is my view that if we are to deal properly with the accounting implications of changing money values, then we must have in front of us a clear analysis of assets on the following lines:

(i) Real or physical.
(ii) Intangibles.
(iii) Monetary claims.

It is my opinion that the whole problem of changing money values *as a question of accounting measurement* should be limited to real or physical assets. There is a plain distinction to be drawn between measurement and policy. In my opinion monetary claims are correctly *measured* at their current value, but if they are inadequate to the level of activity that a particular enterprise is attempting, then as a matter of policy funds should be brought into the business either by retention or borrowing to cope with the situation. If

---

[1] Cf. *The Measurement of Profit*, p. 68 (Oxford University Press, 1949).

company accounting is to be ideal, therefore, the measurement questions associated with changing money values should be restricted to real or physical assets. I quote from some comments which I made in 1948 and which I still see no particular reason to change:

> The essence of the accounting problem, as related to *homogeneous* measurements of capital and income, is largely centred upon those costs applied to *real* assets (as distinct from what might be called natural financial claims), which are carried over from one accounting period to another as short-term and long-term charges against the future operations of continuing enterprises. Somehow we must strive to get the suspense entries appearing in our balance sheets which measure employed capital, on the same plane of reference. Somehow we must reasonably attempt the same thing with our profit and loss accounts which measure periodic income. Many of us are convinced that the answer lies in the virtual restatement of carried-over costs in terms of current standards of money value. The problem is not one of keeping pace with the purchasing power of money for all purposes, neither does it involve any departure from the objectively dependable basis of accounting record in terms of original costs. It is merely a question of converting those original costs, which are out of time relationship, into current costs, in order that in our statements of measurement all significant entries shall rest on a homogeneous basis.[1]

28. Most accountants will want to know the manner in which the analysis I have indicated above is to be applied to particular assets appearing in the balance-sheets of companies. I would answer the type of question that I should expect to be raised in some such terms as the following. Intangibles, such as Goodwill, depend upon organizing ability and the maintenance of income. In my opinion they have little or no value until they are in fact realized. Therefore there can be no question of maintaining goodwill by any mere device of accounting measurement. Debtors, cash, and liabilities all fall within the class which I would designate monetary claims. Accordingly they do not create any problem of accounting measurement. Investments are also more or less monetary claims; nevertheless, quoted investments do have a market value. I should,

[1] *The Accountant*, 11 Sept. 1948.

therefore, like to see quoted investments stated in the balance-sheets of companies at their market value, and for this purpose I would pass valuation adjustments through a Capital Reserve Account. I expect to be asked what I would do with shares in subsidiary companies. Again, I should like to see these valued on a net assets basis at each accounting date and valuation changes dealt with in much the same manner as for any other investments. I should assume from this that subsidiary company balance-sheets would be consistent with that of their parent company, and so record current values. Fixed assets are usually the real assets. I incline to the view that an inventory of fixed assets should be repriced at current costs (i.e. the costs at the accounting date) of specific assets suitably modified to eliminate temporary fluctuation due to speculative, seasonal, or exceptional influences. I should have thought that most accounting entities would be able to maintain their own indexes, for although it may be difficult to determine the current costs of particular items of equipment it should not prove impossible to arrive at a reasonable approximation for main groups of fixed assets. There is here a clear case for a central capital goods index. An alternative suggestion would require indexes to be maintained by trade associations. In any case enterprises dealing in capital goods ought to know what the last cost is, inasmuch as this will be included in their stock valuations. On the subject of building prices, perhaps some resort might be made to revised rating valuations. It is possible that a central machinery index may be available. In any case the critical requirement is to revalue physical fixed assets at the accounting date in order to measure the amount of depreciation at the current price level which is to be charged to the operating account. In so far as technical mechanics are concerned, the repriced cost of fixed assets, less accumulated depreciation to the beginning of the accounting period on this repriced basis, should be compared with the original cost written-down value. The difference will represent the valuation adjustment which should be passed through to the price change account, an account which, in my view, is best shown among the capital reserves. Current depreciation would then be deducted to arrive at the written-down value on a current cost basis. It is my

view that bygones must be bygones, and the past provisions for
depreciation will only be inadequate if they have been invested in
depreciated monetary claims. If this situation has arisen the defi-
ciency should be dealt with as a policy reserve and not as a matter of
measurement. I add one last point: Excess provisions arising from
falling values should be taken to the credit of the operating account
in exactly the same way as the difference between under provisions
were debited to the same account. As soon as the credit balance on
the price change account has been exhausted no further transfers
should be made, and depreciation accounting will have to revert
to an original cost basis if contributed money capital is to be
preserved.

29. I touch on the question of inventories and I would like to
repeat what I said at a recent course in Cambridge in very simple
explanation of what is meant by the economic expression, 'inventory profit or loss', and for this purpose I engaged in some abstractions. Assume an enterprise which begins and ends its accounting
period with identical quantities of identical stocks. Assume that
the bases of valuation are those of more or less traditional accounting practice (that is, first cost or lower market value), that stocks
are frequently and regularly turned over in their entirety, and that
the enterprise has encountered substantial short-period increases
in the buying prices of its stocks. In these circumstances it should
be clear to all of us that the carrying value of the closing stocks
will be greater than the carrying value of the opening stocks,
despite the fact that they are identical in quantity and kind. This
means that the difference between the two valuations will form
part of the accounting measure of profit. It is this part which is
called inventory profit. I leave it to you to work out for yourselves
what is meant by inventory loss.

Now, although my assumptions may seem unreal, they are not
so far distant from that situation in which by far the greater part of
a company's investment in inventories is virtually a fixed asset,
because it is essential to the *continuation* of the company's operations at an effective level of output. You will recognize that this
situation is *not* uncommon. I am myself convinced that inventory
profits and losses are substantial in periods beset by noticeable

price changes, and this circumstance is peculiarly relevant to those enterprises which *have to carry* heavy inventories. If selling margins happen to be low we can easily see what a disconcerting and distorting influence is brought to bear on the accounting measurement of operating income. Moreover, as some writers never tire of telling us, an element of inventory profit is itself represented in the closing inventory valuation. Plainly this is not yet a realized profit available for *immediate* distribution; nevertheless it will almost certainly involve an increased tax liability. Again, I would like to reiterate the conclusions I came to in the course of the discussion to which I have referred. In so far as the major portion of the inventory of an enterprise *does* constitute a fixed asset necessary to the *continuation* of effective operations, it is my view that it should be classified as such in the balance-sheet. In this case, it also seems to me that inventory profits or losses should be excluded from the measurement of operating income, but I add the proviso, perhaps only very exceptionally required, that a loss must be recovered by appropriation out of either previously accumulated price-change profits (the usual means), or current income, where not to do so would do anything to impair the protection of contributed money-capital implied by legal sanction. I also wish to make clear my view that where inventories can be liquidated without doing hurt to the long-run stability and operating activity of an enterprise, then there is little need to bother with inventory profits or losses, for then the inventories themselves are little more than speculative asset claims. The essence of the inventory problem resides in the fundamental distinction between fixed and speculative holdings. The measurement of current inventory costs does not present great difficulties, and there is a clear case for *pegging* opening and closing valuations in those cases where the physical content constitutes a *continuing* investment necessary to activity. Surely no one can urge that accounting practices should countenance the inclusion of unrealized windfall gains within a customary measurement of operating income. I add one further comment. A change in the design of plant output may bring additional inventories into the continuing investment category. These additions should be financed either out of savings or borrowing, because they constitute *real* asset formation. If for any reason this revised level of inventory investment is drawn upon without any conscious change in the scale of output, then provision must be made to cover its replacement in conditions of rising current costs[1] if continuity is to be financially safeguarded.[2]

30. On the mechanics of inventory valuation I do not myself greatly favour the L.I.F.O. method because of the balance-sheet undervaluation which this involves. In point of fact I favour a method of maintaining the lower of opening and closing stocks. This will allow stock reserves, debits, or credits, to be passed through the profit and loss account according to the difference between the pricing out of opening and closing inventories. Alternatively I would rehabilitate the method of base stocks. In either case the intention is to remove inventory profits or losses.

31. Having dealt with the valuation issues affecting the revenue accounts of companies, I would now like to pass on to the general question of the form of company accounts. I start with the operating section of the profit and loss account, and would like to declare from the outset my view that there is no particular merit in limiting this account to a statement of the trading profit to be more or less adjusted by a number of items calling for special disclosure. The best of the public corporations in America have long ago discarded this approach and, in point of fact, they are only too anxious to give details of their turnover and other operating incomings as a sign of their effectiveness. Equally they are prepared to disclose the main details of their operating outgoings. It is my view that a simple operating account could be designed in primary terms to give the major part of the information which anybody is likely to require from company accounts. Most of you will be familiar enough with its traditional form and I do not think there is any great necessity to lay it out again here. What I would like to see is a redesigned form to give a reasonably clear idea of the output value added by a

---

[1] Equivalent to current costs less liquidated carrying cost.

[2] Cf. *Accounting Principles*, vol. ii, No. 4, 'Accounting Research', Oct. 1951, pp. 359–61.

company as achieved through its input allocations of labour and capital. I incline to the view that a redesigned operating account in the manner I am about to put forward to you would give the operating profit arising from the particular piece of economic activity undertaken by the company—a most important figure for everyone concerned. Although simple in structure, I think it is an account which can be made to fit in with all reasonable disclosure requirements. I set it out opposite.

32. You will at once notice that, so far as traditional accounting practice is concerned, this form is revolutionary. It is not so revolutionary to economists, since it brings out the concept of value added by the organization and utilization of production factors in operating activity. As you will know, this concept is a familiar feature of census returns. It is a concept which is readily susceptible to accounting treatment. Purchases of goods and services adjusted for changes in inventories (a device for carrying over unmatched costs from one accounting period to another), when brought within the net of the operating activity of a period of account, are transformed into sales of goods and services at the values placed upon them in the market. Nevertheless there is one major problem which has to be faced in giving accounting significance to the value added concept. I have already touched upon inventory profits or losses which are of the nature of windfall gains and losses bearing no direct relation to operating activity. In addition there are other windfall gains and losses. As you will know, these are usually the outcome of marked changes in those prices which directly affect the purchases or sales of goods and services entering into the calculation of the product of activity. If we are relating the value added to the factor costs of activity, then these are windfall profits or losses which should be removed and dealt with separately in the appropriation account. It is probable, however, that this would make for too many complications in ordinary company accounting. I therefore suggest that, as a start, we should consider the form I have proposed—deal with depreciation on a current cost basis and maintain inventories at their *real* level. Operating profit is itself a test of effectiveness, since it measures the difference between the value added by reason of the

OPERATING ACTIVITY:

Input allocations				*Output value added*	
I. LABOUR—Wages and salaries and social insurance contributions				I. NET SALES of goods and services† . .	x
(i) Direct or operative . . .	x			II. MINUS net purchases of goods and services varying with output‡.	x
(ii) Ancillary . .	x	x			x
(iii) Selling and distribution . .		x		III. CHANGES in inventories§	x
(iv) Administration and management	x	x			x
II. CAPITAL				IV. MINUS net purchases of goods and services related to productive facilities, *not* varying with output . .	x
(i) Rents (imputed or actual)					
1. Factory. .	x				
2. Warehouse and salesroom .	x				
3. Office . .	x	x			
(ii) Depreciation of *real* assets, measured in terms of end-period prices*	x				
(iii) Interest on *real* assets (excluding buildings), employed during the period of account, and measured in terms of end-period prices .	x	x			
		x			
III. OPERATING SURPLUS .		x			
		x		Total Value Added .	x

NOTES:

*I am aware that this conceptual measurement involves serious practical difficulties.

† After deducting returns, allowances, discounts, and bad debts.

‡ After deducting returns, allowances, and discounts. Indirect taxes are included in purchases.

§ Subject to valuation adjustments.

Net Purchases of Goods and Services. A separate indication might be required of provisions to meet liabilities for goods and services, not determined at the accounting date with substantial accuracy.

The Input allocation under the heading of Administration and Management might require specific separate disclosures in respect of the remuneration and benefits of directors.

company's activity and the total inputs of labour and capital which it has engaged to secure that added value. Efficiency ratios using operating profit suggest themselves in the following terms:

1. Operating profit as a function of the current value of the *real* assets employed in the activity.
2. Operating profit per unit of output.
3. Operating profit as a function of total input factor costs.
4. Operating profit as a function of the product (i.e. the value added).

33. It will be noticed that, under the heading of Capital, we meet a rather unusual entry for interest on real assets employed during the period of account, measured in terms of end-period prices. The intention behind this entry is to cover the economic conception of profit in the limiting terms of the reward of risk-bearing and organization. The reward of management is properly looked upon as a labour input. The interest on borrowed money is excluded from operating debits on the grounds that it properly forms part of the interest on capital employed. It seems, therefore, that there is much to be said for an accounting disclosure which reflects the economic distinction between the reward of capital and the reward of risk-bearing and organization. As a first start to the statement of this view, interest on borrowed money is relegated as a purely financial transaction to the Appropriation Account. In order that the measurement of operating profit should conform to its economic conception it is necessary to put through a debit for interest on real assets employed in the operating account and to carry an equivalent credit into the Appropriation Account. In this view the interest charged is related to the real assets employed in the working of the company. I know that there are difficulties in the way of determining the rate. Even so I should not have thought it was too great an approximation to use a rate equivalent to the average yield on the market values of gilt-edged securities at accounting dates.

34. I append a form of Appropriation Account. You will see that it is the purpose of this account to measure the retained income of a company after bringing to account its financial incomings and

disposing of its financial outgoings. The income of the entity is then subject to transfers in respect of direct taxation and dividends. The retained income of the period is brought down to the second section of the Appropriation Account, in which transfers to and withdrawals from reserves and provisions also appear. By bringing in the retained income at the beginning of the period we finally arrive at the retained income to be carried forward to the next period; this is a revenue reserve item appearing in the balance-sheet. It is the purpose of the Appropriation Account to measure the company's total income from all sources, to deal with the amount of its income which it is required to transfer away (a) by means of taxes, and (b) by means of dividend distribution to shareholders, so as to arrive at the retained income of the period of account. The second part of the account merely deals with certain disclosure provisions in relation to reserves and shows the accumulated saving of the company.

APPROPRIATION ACCOUNT

I. Interest on borrowed money . . .	I. Operating profit .
II. Direct income taxes .	II. Interest on real assets employed . .
III. Dividends paid and proposed . . .	III. Income from investments . . .
IV. Retained income .	
V. Transfers to reserves	IV. Retained income of the period . . .
VI. Retained income carried forward to next period . . .	V. Withdrawals from reserves and provisions
	VI. Retained income brought forward from last period .

35. Information on the source and use of industrial finance would be greatly facilitated if companies could be induced to publish a summary account of their capital incomings and outgoings, much as the best companies do in America. It would also explain

balance-sheet changes. I use the technical name by calling it a resting account and suggest the following form:

RESTING ACCOUNT

Capital outgoings	Capital incomings
I. Real asset formation (including changes in inventories) . .	I. Retained income .
II. Movements in deferred assets . . .	II. Depreciation of real assets and other internal operating provisions
III. Lending . . .	III. New capital . .
IV. Net purchase of existing securities . .	IV. Borrowing . .
V. Changes in current net indebtedness . .	V. Movements in deferred liabilities . . .
VI. Changes in monetary balances . . .	

36. I turn to the balance-sheet. As I have said before, I regard this document as the accounting means of employing certain valuation conventions to measure entity wealth, capital and reserves, net worth, or whatever expression you choose to select for what is nothing more than a measure of capital. In a general sense the fundamental and ultimate purpose of a balance-sheet is to measure capital and to show its set-up in the form of integral aggregates of assets and liabilities. Whilst it is important to indicate ownership claims on capital, they are secondary to its primary measurement. In the context of the valuation concepts I have already discussed, this would require that real assets were brought into account at balance-sheet dates on the same basis as current assets, i.e. at their current costs at the accounting date. It is probable that this view of the matter is as yet too advanced for company legislation, and while I have indicated my preference for a measurement of profit which carries in depreciation on a current cost basis and which maintains the physical content of inventories, I would not necessarily commit myself to the logical view of the balance-sheet as a measurement of capital, in the sense I have indicated, in interim company legislation. I would think that great advances had been made if income was correctly measured. I would then regard the

balance-sheet as a document to illustrate the stewardship of contributed money capital and savings. Such increased amounts of depreciation over original cost as the measurement of real profit would require, together with stock reserves, I should prefer to deal with in a price-change account to be included in the balance-sheet reserves. Accountants usually denote the money valuation contents of an ordinary balance-sheet in terms of what they are accustomed to regard as a fundamental equation of accounts. It is explained in simple terms, as follows:

Real Assets, plus Asset claims, minus Liability claims, equals Capital. This points to a fundamental classification informing the structure of all balance-sheets, which needs emphasizing. It brings out the pivotal significance of monetary claims for the process of consolidation and it isolates a measure of real wealth. Asset and liability claims can be conveniently brought within the categories of long term, short term, and deferred. Real assets will ordinarily comprise the fixed assets of accounting terminology and inventories. I would, therefore, like to deal with fixed assets in terms of:

1. Real or physical assets.
2. Deferred expenditure benefiting the activities of future accounting periods.
3. Intangible assets.
4. That part of the inventories of the company required to ensure the continuation of its effective operations.

The balance of the inventories may be regarded as speculative and included as a monetary claim in the short-term department of those claims. All other balance-sheet aggregates are virtually financial and, as I have already said, these are conveniently and concisely categorized as long term, short term, and deferred. Whatever additional disclosure items may be required, either by statute or otherwise, I have a preference for such descriptions of claims, whether asset or liability; they seem to me simple, clear, and universal. I therefore suggest the following form of balance-sheet adapted to a minimum of disclosure requirements which legislation may regard as necessary:

BALANCE-SHEET

I. AUTHORIZED CAPITAL (detailed) . . ——	**I. FIXED ASSETS**
II. ISSUED CAPITAL AND CAPITAL RESERVES .	1. (i) Real or physical x
1. Issued (detailed) . x	(ii) Minus accumulated provisions for depreciation x
2. Capital Redemption Reserve Fund . x	—
3. Premium Accounts x	x x
4. Price Change account . . . x	2. Deferred expenditure benefiting the activities of future accounting periods x
5. Capital reserves . x	3. Intangible . . x x
—	—
x	4. Standard inventories . . . x
III. REVENUE RESERVES AND RETAINED INCOME . x	— x
— x	**II. LONG-TERM ASSET CLAIMS**
IV. LONG-TERM LIABILITY CLAIMS (with a separate disclosure of those which are secured) . x	1. Investments (with a separate disclosure of trade, quoted, and unquoted investments) . . x
V. SHORT-TERM LIABILITY CLAIMS AND PROVISIONS (with a separate disclosure of that part which is secured).	2. Lending (with a separate disclosure of loans to employees, directors, or officers). . x
1. Short-term borrowing . . . x	— x
2. Creditors and accrued expenses . x	**III. SHORT-TERM ASSET CLAIMS**
3. Provisions . . x	1. Speculative inventories . . . x
4. Proposed dividends x	2. Debtors . . x
5. Current tax liabilities . . . x	3. Bank and Cash balances . . x
— x	— x
VI. DEFERRED LIABILITIES x	
—	—
x	x
—	—

NOTES

1. Particulars of share options.
2. Arrears of fixed cumulative dividends.
3. Charges on the company's assets to secure other people's liabilities.

4. Contingent liabilities.
5. Estimated capital expenditure commitments.
6. Market value of quoted investments.
7. Basis of conversion of foreign currencies.

It might be convenient to classify the real or physical assets under the sub-heading of structures and equipment.

37. The balance-sheet should be signed by at least two directors and I should prefer to see the auditors' report adapted to the new British form. For the sake of completeness I give an example of it:

We have obtained all the information and explanations which to the best of our knowledge and belief were necessary for the purposes of our audit. In our opinion proper books of account have been kept by the Company so far as appears from our examination of those books. We have examined the above balance-sheet and annexed profit and loss account which are in agreement with the books of account. In our opinion and to the best of our information and according to the explanations given to us the said accounts give the information required by the Companies' Act, 1948, in the manner so required and the balance-sheet gives a true and fair view of the state of the Company's affairs as at .... and the profit and loss account gives a true and fair view of the (profit/loss) for the year ended on that date.

Whenever possible in the accounts the corresponding figures should be stated for the immediately preceding financial period. I hope I have succeeded in indicating such a design for published company accounts as will portray the best part of that information which shareholders, creditors, economists, statisticians, and the general public may require from them.

38. If I may, I should like to close the provocations implicit in this paper on a forward note. You will remember I remarked earlier that in the long run there is little lost but much gained by disclosing the economic status of those organized entities which substantially contribute to the wants and add to the wealth of enlightened nations. This view springs from a conviction that our understanding of the mechanics of economic stability at a high level of activity must, in part, depend upon a study of empirical

measures. Accounting provides some of these measures. These accounting measures, in their turn, should arouse reflections upon interpretations which pass beyond the boundaries of measurement in subordination of quantity to quality. It is at this point that the accountant and the economic statistician conjoin.

3

ACCOUNTING AND STATISTICAL RELATIONSHIPS

The substance of a paper given on 20 July 1952 at a conference of The Association of Incorporated Statisticians in St. Hugh's College, Oxford

ACCOUNTING AND STATISTICAL RELATIONSHIPS

'The fact that changes in our material universe can be predicted—that they are subject to mathematical law—is the most significant thing about it, for mathematical law is a concept of the mind, and from the existence of mathematical law we infer that our minds have access to something akin to themselves that is in or behind the universe.'

Eddington's Principle in the Philosophy of Science,
by Sir Edmund Whittaker, p. 34
(Cambridge University Press, 1951)

1. I begin by telling you that I have prepared this paper from the standpoint of an accountant who is looking forward to the development of a subject in which he believes. I style it accounting and statistical relationships because I have a strong feeling that the application of mathematical methods to accounting forms will find its most fruitful source in that area where the superior questions are those of interpretation and prediction. Perhaps I should mention that in an amateur way I have toyed with this prospect for some time now without reaching any precise conclusions. The defect lies in my own training; nevertheless, I can see that on any mathematical plane of reference accounting information, as at present displayed, is not very tidily conceived, and I hope that if I address myself to this problem, you gentlemen, with your specialized equipment, will be able to guide the subject several stages forward.

2. To affirm my faith, I should like to make use of the following quotations taken from a lecture on accounting research which I gave in the University of Sydney in October 1949.

I cannot help feeling that the world of ideas to which accounting research will be led, will eventually show itself with some of the qualities of mathematical theory. Indeed, it is a little puzzling to me that mathematical theory is so lightly attached to the present art of accounting. . . . I believe that some mathematical or statistical application will sharpen accounting concepts. Moreover, it will give precision to accounting relationships and should be pursued. A great deal of work still remains to be done on accounting ratios. In particular we need to discover if there is any correlation between different items in the operating statements of entities within like industrial groups.[1]

3. Despite this affirmation, I think it well to take note of one or two warnings. At one extreme there are some remarks made by Little which are not without relevance in the special context of our own immediate subject. He says: 'The myth we are concerned with is the myth that the economic calculus is an exact description of some possible world. There are signs that economic doctrines have tended to harden into dogmas which are defended with religious fervour, and that *laissez-faire* is not the only economic creed which has evoked an almost metaphysical awe.'[2] At the other extreme is a point of view which maintains that an experienced person, intimate with the data, can solve most business problems, involving numbers, by the use of quite simple methods. Experiment and speculation may require more finished techniques, but these should not be used as a matter of course to solve any and every problem with a statistical bent.

4. I think we all recognize that the great majority of the problems which confront us in the daily run of business affairs have to do with numbers, with numbers standing for some kind of quantitative measurement. The idea that a carefully chosen sample of measurements can be made to reveal the properties of its total population forms one of the principal domains of statistical reasoning.

5. I do not myself think that an understanding of sampling methods is likely to lead to any major developments in accounting theory, such as are contemplated by those who pursue accounting research. Nevertheless, I can see that particular business problems may arise which depend for their solution upon the ascertainment of aggregates which cut across and may even lie outside the formal categories of customary patterns of account. In these cases special

[1] *The Accounting Mission*, pp. 61 and 63 (Melbourne University Press, 1951; Great Britain: Cambridge University Press).
[2] *A Critique of Welfare Economics*, by I. M. D. Little, p. 259 (Oxford: at the Clarendon Press, 1950).

extractions would be laborious and expensive, and there is every-thing to be said for the application of sampling methods which avoid biased estimates. But for the most part these are largely problems of control and of mechanics.

6. A certain amount has been written about sampling methods as applied to auditing test checks. In this context I must record my view that fraudulent entries, or a lack of entries presupposing fraud, in books of account, usually turn up when and where they are unsuspected, with all the characteristics of the unexpected. I am, therefore, sufficiently old-fashioned to prefer the examina-tion of a selected series of entries which is both complete and continuous in itself, in order to secure that nothing at random has matured within that range. I am inclined to think that the selection of the period is more a matter of auditing experience than of technical analysis, though I do see that a sequential sampling plan used systematically has advantages where the records of large industrial entities are made the subjects of continuous audits. The trouble is that apart from mere mechanist slips, slips which should be virtually non-existent in these days of highly developed record-ing, no error is really acceptable to an auditor as an *error* until its motive has been thoroughly probed. It is, therefore, my view that the real future of accounting theory in association with statistics lies not so much in sampling and such-like techniques as in a mature development and understanding of the relatedness of aggregate categories in formal patterns of account. As things are at present, relationships in accounting theory are limited to simple ratios between categories. I cannot but think that such ratios by them-selves are far too simple to be wholly adequate, more particularly if we are seeking to quantify aggregate expectations. As most of us know, these expectations have deep implications both for the part of an enterprise and the whole of an economy at large.

7. I fear conservative accountants very much incline to the view that there are few, if any, mathematical properties to be deduced from accounting statements. They are a little apt to withdraw from the principles of quantitative measurement by taking refuge in such legal implications as are denoted by the notion of steward-ship. Although it has practical advantages I have never been very

satisfied with this approach to accounting theory. It has been commented upon on more than one occasion that measurement is the most powerful of all scientific tools because it lends precision to qualitative concepts of order and makes available all the resources of mathematics.

8. A few years ago I wrote that 'accountancy may be thought of as a systematic record of the working of the economic structure of society in terms of monetary symbols. As it takes on and develops notions of economic order, it gradually points to what *should be* by accuracy of statement in regard to what *is*.'[1] It seems to me that herein lies the key to the purpose of my present subject. Accuracy of statement in regard to what *is* requires a relentless pursuit after validity and accuracy of conceptual measurements, especially where real resources are concerned. If accurate measurement is validly sought and attained then the next step becomes a question of form. Thereafter it ought to be one of the vital functions of accounting to show as simply as possible how the epitomized transactions of a period and at a point in time are interconnected.

9. This is only another way of saying that accountants must delve after and settle the accounting principles of both measurement and form, before their accounts *can* be utilized statistically. I am not sure which I rate the higher, measurement or form. Both are matters of essential consequence, and if accuracy of measurement seems the more axiomatic in the special context of our present discussion there can be little question that right structure and form are receptive of right matter. I hope you will bear with me if I seem to be a little speculative in what I am about to say. Schrödinger has observed that form, not substance, is the fundamental concept. He says that 'it is beyond doubt that the question of "sameness", of identity, really and truly has no meaning'.[2] Although he was writing with special reference to physics, I think that those accountants and statisticians who ponder the fundamental principles of their own skills can draw on, or borrow from, a great deal of Schrödinger's

[1] *Precision and Design in Accountancy*, p. 19 (Gee & Co. (Publishers) Ltd., 1947).
[2] *Science and Humanism, Physics in our time*, by E. Schrödinger, p. 18 (Cambridge University Press, 1951).

ideas. I ask you to consider the philosophy implicit in the following series of quotations. 'It is clearly the peculiar *form* or *shape* (German: *Gestalt*) that raises the identity beyond doubt, not the material content.'[1] '. . . we can see—how in palpable bodies, composed of many atoms, individuality arises out of the structure of their composition, out of shape or form, or organization, as we might call it in other cases. The identity of the *material*, if there is any, plays a subordinate role.'[2] 'The *new* idea is that what is permanent in these ultimate particles or small aggregates is their shape and organization. . . . When you come to the ultimate particles constituting matter, there seems to be no point in thinking of them again as consisting of some material. They are, as it were, *pure shape*, nothing but shape; what turns up again and again in successive observations is this shape, not an individual speck of material.'[3] 'Probably we cannot ask for more than just adequate pictures capable of synthesizing in a comprehensible way all observed facts and giving a reasonable expectation on new ones we are out for.'[4] '. . . quantum laws, though they leave the single event undetermined, predict a quite definite *statistics* of events, when the same situation occurs again and again.'[5]

10. You will gather it is my view that statistical relationships are properties of form, not of substance. The form must be knowable before it can be correctly set, and in accounting this depends upon the choice of right categories. I think we must agree that interpretation and prediction depend upon a due regard for order, and that right order depends upon the selection of right categories as well as the proper measurement of such transactions as fall to be included in those categories. The accounts of epitomized transactions are best limited by comparatively few categories. The intention is to secure significant measures with such an economy of detail that they are easily understood and yield valid conclusions. Any form of account ought to be easily and readily susceptible to analysis. Accounts which are both simple *and* fundamental in design are likely to yield better inferences than more complex ones.

11. In the more recent history of accounting the qualitative

---

[1] Op. cit., p. 19.   [2] Ibid., p. 20.   [3] Ibid., p. 21.
[4] Ibid., p. 24.   [5] Ibid., p. 61.

concept of order has been investigated, on a pragmatic level, before the quantitative concept of measurement. Nevertheless, the concept of measurement is beginning to worry accountants. This is all to the good because, as Kuznets has observed, the growing measurability and practice of accounting in everyday life is making for a growing body of statistics. So far as the present subject is concerned I think the sequence of discussion is order, measurement, and the codification of aggregate categories into formulae. All accounting trends depend upon a time series of formally related accounts, prepared for specific periods and marked off at definite points in time. Formal accuracy and measurability on the same plane of reference are essential if we are to safeguard such statistical relationships as are inferrable from aggregate categories in accounts.

12. I regard all accounts as frames of aggregates, and in this respect I pass on to what I think are the fundamental notions of order, and I call them the identities of structure and the identities of form. As for the identities of structure you will know that a substantial part of economics is brought under discussion and explained by reference to national aggregates of income and expenditure and their interrelation. It seems that the problems which confront economists in the applied fields of income and expenditure, and the study of wealth, necessitate certain empirical constructions which only attain reliable proportions when they are made to fit into the self-checking pattern of a double-entry system of accounts. This pattern must conform to certain primary economic concepts which in their simplest form are independently related in a closed economy in two ways. Thus, if Y = Income, C = Consumption, S = Saving, and I = Investment or asset formation, then

$$Y = C + S, \text{ and}$$
$$S = I.$$

These are the Keynesian identities of any accounting structure relevant to a nation's transactions, and the primary economic concepts as so formally related give birth to a series of fundamental accounts which are just as relevant for firms or companies as for the nation as a whole.

13. I apologize for treading some old ground, but I have always regarded it as a matter of considerable consequence that accounting forms should be tied to the two economic concepts of periodic income and wealth. When these are looked at in terms of the Keynesian identities I have cited, it is easy to see that income is devoted to consumption expenditure and saving, with saving as the source of asset formation, and that wealth implies a store of assets. To my way of thinking there can be little question that this approach gives rise to some formal principles of accounting design which are expressed in the following series of fundamentally related accounts.

    i. To measure periodic income.

    ii. To show the transfer and disposition of that income.

    iii. To explain the application of retained income or saving, its effect upon wealth, and capital changes.

    iv. To measure and portray those resources which together make up the wealth of an entity.

Such accounts are variously denoted as:

    (a) Profit and Loss, or Operating and Income.

    (b) Appropriation and Outlay.

    (c) Sources and Uses of Funds, or Capital Reconciliation, or Resting.

    (d) Balance-sheet.

14. I now turn to some simple identities of form, and by way of introduction I make the claim that accounting ought to ensure reasonable accuracy and completeness in the measurement of aggregate variable categories. Every accountant knows that accounts must balance, and this by itself is a statistical check which indicates some fundamental limits on economic behaviour. Income is very largely generated by reason of exchange between production entities. Exchange is a double-sided affair establishing an equality of inputs and outputs, the genesis of double-entry recording. Thus epitomized transactions as displayed in accounts are the results of economic processes which in themselves are balancing, and this explains the derivation of accounting identities of form.

Nevertheless, it is important to remember that accounting equations do *not* of themselves necessarily reveal causal relationships except in so far as some of the variables determining economic activity are themselves brought under measurable categories in accounts. But they do go a long way in aiding our understanding of probable causal agents. At any rate it can certainly be said that such variables as do constitute categories in accounts are themselves complete and consistent within the framework of whatever entity of account is in point.

15. I set out below the structural framework and categories of a simple series of accounts. You will notice that each account can be expressed in terms of an identity of form which imposes its own constraint.

OPERATING ACTIVITY

Input allocations			*Output value added*		
A. LABOUR—Wages and salaries and social insurance contributions			D. OUTPUT		
1. Operative	x		1. Sales of goods and services	x	
2. Ancillary	x	x	2. *Minus* Purchases of goods and services varying with output	x	x
3. Selling and distribution		x			
4. Administration and management	x	x	ΔE. Changes in inventories		x
B. CAPITAL					x
1. Rents (imputed or actual)	x		F. MINUS Purchases of goods and services related to productive facilities *not* varying with output		x
2. Depreciation of *real* assets measured in terms of end-period prices	x				
3. Interest on *real* assets (excluding buildings) employed during the period of account, and measured in terms of end-period prices	x	x			
C. OPERATING INCOME	x				
	x		Total value added	x	

$$A+B+C = D \pm \Delta E - F$$

INCOME

G. Interest on borrowed money	x	C. Operating income . . x
H. Entity income . .	x	B_3. Interest on real assets employed x
		I. Financial income . . x
	x	x

$$G+H = C+B_3+I.$$

APPROPRIATION

J. Income transfers:		H. Entity income . . x
1. Direct taxation .	x	
2. Dividends and withdrawals . . .	x x	
K. Retained income . .	x	
	x	x

$$J+K = H$$

RESTING

ΔL. Real asset formation .	x	K. Retained income . . x
ΔE. Changes in inventories .	x	B_2. Depreciation of real assets x
ΔM. Real asset valuation adjustments . . .	x	ΔS. Capital valuation adjustments x
ΔN. Movements in deferred expenditures . .	x	ΔT. Movements in deferred liabilities . . . x
ΔO. Lending . . .	x	ΔU. New capital . . . x
ΔP. Net purchases of financial investments . . .	x	ΔV. Borrowing . . . x
ΔQ. Changes in short-term claims . . .	x	
ΔR. Changes in money balances . . .	x	
	x	x

$$\Delta L+\Delta E+\Delta M+\Delta N+\Delta O+\Delta P+\Delta Q+\Delta R = K+B_2+\Delta S+\Delta T+\Delta U+\Delta V$$

BALANCE-SHEET

V. Long-term claims— borrowing				LMB. Real assets—Fixed			
V. Opening	.	. x		L. Opening	.	. x	
ΔV. Of the period	.	x	x	ΔL. Formation	.	. x	
						M. x	
T. Deferred liabilities				ΔM₁. Valuation adjustments	.	. . x	
T. Opening	.	. x				x	
ΔT. Movements	.	. x	x	B₂. Depreciation	.	x	x
USK. Capital				EM. Real assets—Inventories			
U. Opening	.	. x		E. Opening	.	. x	
ΔU. New capital	.	x		ΔM₂. Valuation adjustments	.	. . x	
		S x		ΔE. Formation	.	. x	x
ΔS. Valuation adjustments	.	. . x		N. Deferred expenditures			
K. Retained income	.	x	x	N. Opening	.	. x	
				ΔN. Movements	.	. x	x
				O. Long-term claims— lending			
				O. Opening	.	. x	
				ΔO. Of the period	.	x	x
				P. Long-term claims— financial investments			
				P. Opening	.	. x	
				ΔP. Of the period	.	x	x
				Q. Net Short-term claims			
				Q. Opening	.	. x	
				ΔQ. Changes	.	. x	x
				R. Money balances	.		
				R. Opening	.	. x	
				ΔR. Changes	.	. x	x
		x					x

$$V \pm \Delta V + T \pm \Delta T + U \pm \Delta U \pm \Delta S \pm K = L \pm \Delta L \pm \Delta M_1 - B_2 + E \pm \Delta M_2 \pm \Delta E +$$
$$N \pm \Delta N + O \pm \Delta O + P \pm \Delta P + Q \pm \Delta Q + R \pm \Delta R$$

Here we have an interconnected system of accounts with an intelligible structure. In this system there are a number of variable aggregate categories which ought to be capable of some degree of correlation.

16. Nevertheless, both the structure and the identities of form only assume reliable proportions if due attention is paid to certain

principles of measurement. It is an axiom of accounting that for the most part business undertakings should be looked upon as continuing enterprises and that as a consequence the operating profit or loss of an accounting period should be derived from and measured by a comparison of the current operating outgoings with the current operating incomings of the period in such a way that the real resources invested in operating assets at the beginning of the period should be preserved at the close of the period. This ordinarily[1] involves an allocation in respect of depreciation of fixed assets based on the current costs of the assets at the accounting date and attention to a record of inventory usage on the same plane of reference. For obvious reasons real resources do not include assets or liabilities represented by money claims, so that the measurement questions associated with changing money values are restricted to real or physical assets. I quote from some comments which I made in 1948 and which I still see no particular reason to change:

The essence of the accounting problem, as related to *homogeneous* measurements of capital and income, is largely centred upon those costs applied to *real* assets (as distinct from what might be called natural financial claims), which are carried over from one accounting period to another as short-term and long-term charges against the future operations of continuing enterprises. Somehow we must strive to get the suspense entries appearing in our balance sheets which measure employed capital, on the same plane of reference. Somehow we must reasonably attempt the same thing with our profit and loss accounts which measure periodic income. Many of us are convinced that the answer lies in the virtual restatement of carried-over costs in terms of current standards of money value. The problem is not one of keeping pace with the purchasing power of money for all purposes, neither does it involve any departure from the objectively dependable basis of accounting record in terms of original costs. It is merely a question of converting those original costs, which are out of time relationship, into current costs, in order that in our statements of measurement all significant entries shall rest on a homogeneous basis.[2]

---

[1] In this context and for the purpose of defining statistical relationships I omit any reference to the legal constraints imposed by company law.

[2] *The Accountant*, 11 Sept. 1948.

As a matter of rough justice and practical expediency, I throw out the suggestion that current costs might be measured by reference to an average of the retail and wholesale price indexes. I recognize that this conversion factor has defects. Nevertheless, it does have the merit of being a broad measure of changing money values. It reaches back well into the past, and is kept up to date by published monthly calculations. Moreover, it is an average of official objective indexes and is therefore independent and authoritative.

17. I hope I have succeeded in making it plain that accounting measures must encompass the effects of changes in the value of money if the identities of structure and of form to which I have referred are not to be mathematically meaningless. Depreciation of real operating assets is an essential imputed constituent of the input allocation for capital in any account of operating activity to measure business income. Entity wealth is made up of real assets and monetary claims, and the problems of accounting classification as well as those of accounting measurement appear in a new light as soon as we recognize the dichotomy between the real and the financial. Thus it is clear that if the concept of operating income is to have meaning then both depreciation and inventory usage must be measured on a scale appropriate to the accounting date for the setting forth of aggregates. Although I have suggested a rough scale of measurement, I do not want it to be thought that I am not alive to the fact that for some firms *real* assets and the manner of their distribution and replacement are of much greater importance than for others.

18. I now turn to the relevance of accounting form to statistical relationships and the first thing I want to notice is that a series of operating accounts, designed as here proposed, when set back in terms of constant prices provide us with appropriate data for a study of the production function relating output to varying combinations of labour and capital inputs. In its simplest form this function can be set up by means of a two-way table, listing on the left-hand side the varying amounts of capital and along the bottom the varying amounts of labour, and by putting into this framework the appropriate outputs. We then have a diagram of past experience, and providing we know something about an output expectation

we may detect those combinations of inputs which the past suggests ought to produce it. In theory the ultimate issue is formally resolved by selecting the minimum cost combination. But this is only one view of an anticipated operating situation, and it is idle to deny that there are hazards. Nevertheless, I feel that much could be gained by a study of the past in this form to aid us in assessing future expectations. Since output is related to the maximization of profit, I should wish to define output for this purpose in terms of sales of goods and services minus purchases of goods and services varying with output plus or minus changes in inventories. But this definition is not free from measurement problems. There is always the possibility of windfall gains and losses which bear no direct relation to operating activity. These are usually the outcome of marked changes in those prices which directly affect the purchases or sales of goods and services entering into the calculation of the product of activity. They tend to promote windfall profits or losses which are (temporarily at least) unrelated to the factor costs of activity. Hence the influence of these changes should be removed from the operating account to be dealt with in the income, appropriation, or resting accounts. You will notice that the operating account as here devised is centred around the 'value added' concept. Thus it is my view that where there has been significant inventory formation on account of work in progress or process, and finished goods, then it is better that this change should be lifted from its conventional valuation in terms of cost to a valuation in terms of market selling prices. The intention of this variation is to secure the homogeneous measurement of output.

19. I pass into the all-important realm of prediction where I think the future of my subject lies, and I suggest that the formal structure of accounts which I have brought to your notice should be looked upon as a model. As with all models, we cannot get away from the underlying assumption that the working of the entity which it represents will continue to function in the future in much the same way as it has done in the past. As we all know, this may be far from true; nevertheless such predictions as we do make from our model should at least serve to high-light exogenous variables

when we are also in possession of empirically devised estimates. For my part, I prefer to work on the basis of an accounting transactional structure because of the constraints which it automatically imposes rather than rely upon a purely number relationship observed between variables which are not themselves integral parts of an intelligible structure. I would express this in rather more sophisticated form by saying that unless there is some philosophical concord between variables there can be no more certain predictable relationships than are established by purely number relationships. When we come to an understanding of the behaviour of accounting variables from a static accounting structure I am inclined to favour simple techniques, such as the single equation least squares regression, because they can be easily comprehended by executives and because such predictions as they lead to are themselves only likely to be used as crude checks on empirically formulated estimates. As Mr. Lomax has recently observed:

in an activity such as econometrics, with its heavy dependence on mathematics, there will always tend to be a conflict between the descriptive and the technical sides of the science. Compromise and reconciliation are urgently needed and in many applications these may ultimately fructify at a point nearer to the crude end of the scale of analysis than at present might be expected. It is a remarkable fact that there are many instances of more convincing results being obtained by crude methods than by elaborate techniques.[1]

This observation is not without point in the context of our own subject.

20. Most firms make empirical estimates of anticipated outputs, and there is everything to be said for contrasting these estimates with a number of statistical checks. If a production plan is given, the combination of labour and capital inputs should be known so that by making use of a production function table built up from past operating accounts it should be possible to predict an output as a standard of reference. Again, it may be possible from past experience to establish some degree of relationship between a firm's output and the national income. Changes in the national income may influence the magnitude of consumer expenditure on

---

[1] *Accounting Research*, Apr. 1952, vol. iii, No. 2, p. 195.

the product according to the income elasticity of the demand for the product. This income elasticity may be determined from past experience. Thus, whenever the consumers' demand for the product has changed less than in proportion to the change in income, the income elasticity of demand is less than unity. If the consumers' demand has changed more than in proportion to the change in income then the income elasticity of demand is greater than unity. By taking such-like factors into account it may be possible to improve the prediction of output as a standard of reference. Yet a third source of information may be established by a time series of outputs to establish the trend. This, too, may be worked into the prediction of output as a standard of reference. Having set the predicted standard this may be compared with the empirically determined estimate in such a way that an acceptable estimate is finally derived.

21. I regard the aggregate for output in the operating account as an independent variable, and I look upon the assessment of operating income as finally determining the pattern of the remaining accounts right down to the balance-sheet measurement of capital employed which again I tend to look upon as an independent variable. Something will be known about the purchases of goods and services related to productive facilities not varying with output, about the charge for administration and management, and about the capital inputs. The remaining variable aggregates in the operating account can be derived by regression analysis from like past period accounts. Thereafter we may set up the whole structure of accounts, on the basis of the identities I have given, for an on-coming period. So we may improve the entrepreneur's budget by the introduction of a few simple statistical techniques. No doubt there is an element of *over simplicity* about all this, particularly when we are reflecting upon capital changes. Nevertheless, most entrepreneurs do survey, as a matter of policy, contemplated capital changes and they more or less know what they intend doing. Accounting estimates must of necessity be set to conform with this policy. But there may be changes in expectations, and unexpected changes in interest rates, the results of which will usually show as capital gains or losses in subsequent historical accounts.

22. Much has been written about standard costing methods in industry.

This system essentially depends upon the economic planning of physical performance. Such planning is primarily the task of the technician, who is required to advance such methods of utilizing resources as will economise materials and effort, achieve high outputs, and control product qualities. The accountant takes over the planned physical standards of the technician, values them in terms of cost, and thereby assigns money measures to preconceived operating performances. It is but a short step to set actual operating costs alongside predetermined costs, and thereafter concentrate attention upon the variations in the hope that such an examination will reveal those points of faulty adjustment which are preventing the realisation of the productive ideal sought.[1]

In principle I regard this way of doing things as but a beginning in the development of expectation accounting. You will notice that the standards are empirically determined. Moreover, I speak from experience when I say that they take some time before they assume the status of normal measures of performance. While I do not deride empirical procedures I think they do need some statistical checking before they are launched into accounting budgets. It seems to me that it ought to be possible to standardize a form of operating account for a department or process in the simplest possible terms so as to minimize the categories in the variable part of that account. If the results of previous and comparable accounting periods are put into the same form it is possible to establish a time series for this particular sphere of activity. A study of the relationships between the variable categories by means of regression analysis both through time and between categories should facilitate predictions for an oncoming period of account. If the predicted standard is out of line with the empirical standard by more than the standard error, then attention is centred upon those exogenous elements in the situation which are unpredictable because there is no repetitive experience to work upon. In this way budgeted standards can be tested and the degree of estimation strengthened at and limited to the anticipated exogenous variables.

23. In cost-accounting work I am inclined to think that

---

[1] *The Accounting Mission,* p. 49.

semi-variable expenditures should be treated as variables. They should move with outputs though not necessarily directly. The statistical notion of limits might be valuable here if changes only occur at intervals. This would give us variability beyond limits and constants within limits. In cost accounting in particular, accountants should never get lost in or over-admire double-entry mechanics without answering some really fundamental questions of interpretation and knowing something about the *via media* as a test of normality.

24. In recent years accountants have developed a system of ratios between aggregate categories in accounts. To my way of thinking some attention must be paid to the principles of measurement and the rigours of form, to which I have drawn attention in this paper, before a valid start can be made along this road. The whole system depends upon the choice of categories and of their ratios as constituting important variables both for classification purposes and for future analysis. First we have to consider the entity or internal interpretation of ratios and second the external interpretation. I do not propose to say much about the latter here except to remark upon the importance of ratio comparisons by size of firm, by rate of growth, by capital structure, by income generation, by degree of liquidity, and so on. Internal interpretation to secure measures of effectiveness is usually based on some such ratios as operating profit to gross output, entity income to capital employed, both before and after direct taxation, cost of sales to gross output, selling expenses to sales, administrative expenses to sales, current assets to current liabilities, fixed assets to capital employed, current liabilities to capital employed, inventories to working capital, working capital to output, annual sales to capital employed, annual sales to working capital, inventory turnover, and the like. In my view the mere construction of these ratios by themselves is inadequate. I think it is essential to set limits within which any given ratio should be held, and to set up a criteria of normal experienced deviation. These are plainly matters for the application of statistical techniques ordered to those ends.

25. Most cost accountants are fond of urging that 'there is no known measurement (and it seems unlikely that there ever will be

one) that accurately reflects, over a short period of time, changes in the overall productivity of a country, industry, or firm'.[1] I cannot but regard this as a little too confident a statement. I know that there are a number of variables to be considered, but I would have thought that many of these variables are correlated to one another. Thus, if we take the case of one entity and consider the following two sets of measures, for this purpose equating product to net output—

Value of product per £ of operative labour cost.
Value of product per £ of real capital investment.
Value of product per head of operative labour.
Value of product per horse-power of plant utilization.

Operating surplus as a function of real assets employed.
Operating surplus per unit of output.
Operating surplus as a function of the total input factor costs.
Operating surplus as a function of the product—

it should be possible to reach expressions of their combination, and it also seems to me that multiple regression analysis could prove useful in this type of study, by suggesting a standard prediction derived from one set of accounting ratios over intervals of time.

There can be little question that accounting would benefit from greater accuracy in the measurement of imputed transactions, particularly in the example of depreciation, and I cannot forbear to quote some comments from Mr. Menzler's presidential address to the Institute of Actuaries in October 1950:

It may be relevant for present purposes to reflect for a moment upon the essential nature of the phenomena which we seek to measure by means *inter alia* of those familiar instruments, the life table and the service table. It is obvious that their underlying characteristics are summed up in the word 'wastage'. The human frame is subject to wear and tear; it requires running repairs; it may completely fail prematurely; or it may last for a full period of life. The forces of attrition are known too well to us all. The wastage of the material resources of civilization offers some

[1] *Measurement of Productivity—Applications and Limitations.* Issued by the Joint Committee of the Institute of Cost and Works Accountants and the Institution of Production Engineers (Gee & Co. (Publishers) Ltd., 1951).

close parallels. Machinery, for example, like other industrial equipment, is also subject to wear and tear and requires running repairs; it may have to be withdrawn from service prematurely because of failure, or possibly because of the onset of the insidious and subtle disease of obsolescence; but it may last for the full budgeted period. As one contemplates the great aggregates of capital equipment of today, one cannot but wonder whether our approaches and methods for the measurement of 'wastage' might not be helpful in the study of the analogous phenomena of wear and tear of capital assets, and of the associated problems of finance and taxation.

26. And lastly, if we think of accounting in terms of the aggregate transactions of society, there are a number of general questions which we should do well to study in terms of the relationships between categories in particular sectors of the social accounts. For example, what is the correlation and the stability of the relationships between corporate enterprise income and saving, between saving and asset expansion, external financing and asset expansion, and so on. This type of inquiry eventually opens out into the whole field of econometrics so that we are led on to a consideration of such problems and statistical inquiries as are discussed in Mr. Richard Stone's monograph on *The Role of Measurement in Economics*.[1] And there I must leave the discussion of my present subject, trusting in the hope that some ideas may have emerged in what is very much a virgin field of inquiry.

[1] Cambridge University Press, 1951.

4

ACCOUNTING FORM

The substance of an address given on Michaelmas, 1952, at a course for Incorporated Accountants in Balliol College, Oxford

ACCOUNTING FORM

'Probably we cannot ask for more than just adequate
pictures capable of synthesizing in a comprehensible
way all observed facts and giving a reasonable expectation on new ones we are out for.'[1]

1. I am to address you this afternoon on the subject of accounting
form. It is a title of my own choosing which when first put forward
was looked upon with some merriment. I propose to introduce it
by commenting upon the philosophical importance of the concept
of form, its relevance to accounting, and then with due regard for
the primary purpose of this course, I will come down to earth and
discuss those forms of accounting statement which I think are best
suited to the surveys and policies of entity managements.

2. Schrödinger in a series of lectures organized by the Dublin
Institute for Advanced Studies and delivered at University College,
Dublin, in February 1950, enunciated what I think is almost a
classical account of scientific effort 'as forming part of man's
endeavour to grasp the human situation'. He spoke as a physicist
dealing with the current conception of matter, but the great significance of his discourse for all of us in our several fields lies in the
clear and precise manner in which he shows that *Form* and *not
Substance* is the fundamental philosophical concept. I am also very
impressed at the notion that 'because of limitations, adequacy
rather than truth is the most that we can ask for in our mental
"models"'.

3. I know that I am speaking to accountants who are very much
caught up in practical affairs. Nevertheless, I believe we should all
do our work very much better if we could occasionally think over
a few fundamental questions which bear upon the things we do
each day, and this type of course should provide that opportunity.
After all, accounts themselves are mental 'models'. I am, therefore,
going to burden you with some quotations from the series of
lectures to which I have already referred. Thus 'it is beyond doubt
that the question of "sameness", of identity, really and truly has no

[1] *Science and Humanism*, by Erwin Schrödinger, p. 24 (Cambridge University
Press, 1951).

meaning'.[1] 'It is clearly the peculiar *form* or *shape* (German: *Gestalt*) that raises the identity beyond doubt, not the material content.'[2] '. . . we can see—how in palpable bodies, composed of many atoms, individuality arises out of the structure of their composition, out of shape or form, or organization, as we might call it in other cases. The identity of the *material*, if there is any, plays a subordinate role.'[3] 'The *new* idea is that what is permanent in these ultimate particles or small aggregates is their shape and organization. . . . When you come to the ultimate particles constituting matter, there seems to be no point in thinking of them again as consisting of some material. They are, as it were, *pure shape*, nothing but shape; what turns up again and again in successive observations is this shape, not an individual speck of material.'[4] Two last ideas and then I shall have done with quotations. '*We must not admit the possibility of continuous observation.* Observations are to be regarded as discrete, disconnected events. Between them there are gaps which we cannot fill in.'[5] '. . . quantum laws, though they leave the single event undetermined, predict a quite definite *statistics* of events, when the same situation occurs again and again.'[6]

4. I fear I may have strained your patience, but what I get out of all this is the predominance of the philosophical concept of form in all fundamental scientific inquiries. Therefore I strongly suspect the same concept has both a primary bearing and a lasting place in those applied techniques which belong to the domain of accounting. I think most of us will admit there is a fair degree of regularity and system in economic life. It is this regularity and system which we have to transpose in terms of accounting forms. As a consequence it is the classification of transactions into formal categories which is important and not necessarily the transactions themselves. The more woolly our notions of regularity and system the more complicated and manifold will be our categories and therefore the more diverse and incomprehensible will be our designs of accounts. The more clear-headed and fundamental our understanding of these things the fewer will be our categories and

[1] Op. cit., p. 18.   [2] Ibid., p. 19.   [3] Ibid., p. 20.
[4] Ibid., p. 21.   [5] Ibid., p. 27.   [6] Ibid., p. 61.

therefore the simpler and more straightforward will be our forms of account. Policy depends upon the interpretations to be derived from these categories and upon a prediction of their probable future magnitudes. Interpretation and prediction are the accompaniments of expectation, or, if you so prefer, budgeting, and it is my view that they rest upon a study and comparison of the magnitudes of like categories over time, in so far as the past can ever be relied upon as a guide to the future.

5. Any form of account, if it is to be worth anything at all, must keep to the same set of classifications, for otherwise there can be but few valid comparisons between periods, or between entities. Moreover, the relationships between categories which we call accounting ratios can have little meaning if we keep on modifying and changing the categories. Standardization of, or uniformity in, the main forms of account seems to me essential, and there does not appear to be much point in continually altering or adding to a layout to meet some transitory purpose which a little thought would show up as a matter of quite trivial import. We must not 'screw up' our accounts. What we must do is to try to think out a few really fundamental forms which are capable of adaptation to all our problems wherever they arise, be it under the headings of management or stewardship.

6. The myth we are concerned with is the myth that accounting complication is an essential component of well thought out accounts. In fact and in experience, there is a strong case for the reverse proposition. It has always seemed to me that a good accountant with a penetrating mind was needed for the preparation of clear and meaningful forms of account. Too many forms and too many categories make for poor comprehension and poor derivations of trends. I have had the experience of telling the same board of directors over and over again, until I tired of the exercise, the meaning and purpose of a series of operating statements designed to reveal volume, calendar, material price, and works controllable variances. I now know that all that was needed in justification or resolution of policy, was a straightforward operating account expressed in terms of originating expectations and actual results, and designed with a minimum of categories in such a way as to

fasten attention upon the main reported causes of variation. To overdo both forms and categories, especially when they are not particularly significant, is to make for distraction rather than concentration. Explanations are matters for report. They may be many and diverse. Variations should be significant, few, and precise, because they are matters of account.

7. Management accounting, to use a pretentious name given to the subject these days, essentially depends upon standard costing and budgeting. As is well known to all of you, standard costing gets to work upon the economic planning of physical performance. The greater part of this planning is the task of the technician, who is required to advance such methods of utilizing resources as will economize materials and effort, achieve high outputs, and control product qualities. The accountant takes over the planned physical standards of the technician, values them in terms of cost, and thereby assigns money measures to preconceived operating performances. As I have said many times before, it is but a short step to set actual operating costs alongside predetermined costs, and thereafter concentrate attention upon the variations in the hope that such an examination will reveal those points of faulty adjustment which are preventing the realization of the production ideals sought.[1] Whilst I do not propose to enter into any mathematical conceptions here, I think I should say that in my view there is a real need for some statistical checking before standard costs are launched into budgets. Checking of such an order will depend upon the detection and standardization of an unsophisticated form of operating account which is adaptable to a department or process, and which can be made the subject of a time series. It will have to be drawn up in the simplest possible terms so as to minimize the variable categories. Those of you who are interested in this statistical or mathematical approach may find something to hold on to in an Oxford paper which I gave to the statisticians in July of this year.[2]

8. Budgeting is a means of bringing together management

---

[1] Cf. *The Accounting Mission*, p. 49 (Melbourne University Press, 1951; Great Britain: Cambridge University Press).

[2] See 'Accounting and Statistical Relationships,' pp. 49–68 of this book.

expectations, of the elements in operating income and their financial implications, within the framework of a balanced set of accounts. In this way it is hoped to reduce the effect of sheer guess-work. Every accountant knows that accounts must balance, and this of itself is a primary check which indicates some fundamental limits on the economic behaviour of an enterprise. Income is very largely generated by reason of exchange between production entities. Exchange is a double-sided affair establishing an equality of inputs and outputs, the genesis of double-entry recording. Thus epitomized transactions as displayed in accounts are the results of economic processes which in themselves are balancing, and this goes some way to explain the derivation of accounting form. It is the merit of a budgeted set of accounts that the estimated expectations of the variable categories have to be consistent within the accounting structure of whatever entity is in point. Thereby limits are set to the over-all movement of a restricted but related number of variables. I think I have said enough to show that methods of standard costing and budgetary control are primarily empirical steps in probability and prediction, and no one can deny that they depend upon an intimate knowledge of a firm's affairs.

9. It is my view that however much we narrow down the spheres of economic activity, whether it be to a particular process or a special department, we are always dealing with the same elemental accounting classifications to aid our understanding of the operation, and to control its results. It does not matter what textbook you pick up on cost or management accounting, you still have to deal with sales of goods and services, purchases of goods and services, changes in inventories, the costs of labour in all its parts, and capital costs whether in the forms of depreciation, rent, or interest. I know that much time is spent on discussion of the methods of cost allocation, but in effect these allocations are nothing more than a breakdown of the expense aggregates of a firm into such component parts as are appropriate to a section of its operations. The elemental categories of expense are still very much the same. Hence, if the primary categories of operating accounts are the same, then I suggest that in principle the *forms* of those accounts, when properly understood, are also very much the same. In strict theory, and as

an aside to this argument, I believe the same proposition holds true for all the fundamental forms of account,[1] but since both cost and management accountings are largely concentrated on operating effectiveness I am purposely limiting myself here to the operating account. You will judge that I believe accounting principles are always the same. I do *not* think that the fundamental concepts of cost accounting or management accounting are different from those of financial or any other type of accounting, any more than I believe that the concept of business income is somehow different from that of personal income. All that is happening is a narrowing down or stepping up of the sphere of operation you choose to look at and interpret. What cost accounting *has* done is to establish the validity of the lesser entity constituted by a process or department as distinct from the legal entity looked upon by financial accounting. By magnifying the lesser entity it has magnified those operating weaknesses which were veiled and obscured by the greater coverage of stewardship accounts. The real problems of both cost and management accounting lie in the choice of and the recording for those basic operating centres within an enterprise which do, in fact, utilize and transform its real resources.

10. The one essential policy of enterprise management is to maximize operating profit, and this usually means maximizing saleable outputs. Such a policy usually carries with it the necessity of minimizing costs, both variable and fixed. This is only another way of saying that all expenditure must be controlled at an effective level. A well-designed operating account should be capable of revealing over time those combinations of labour and capital inputs which maximize output, the production function, as economists call it. The notion of output is important because in net terms it draws attention to the value added to originating goods and services by operating processes. The value added by successive stages of production can be so accounted as to indicate some decisive factors to be minimized, e.g. freight costs in proportion to the value added by a manufacturing process. The form of the

---

[1] I here refer to the Appropriation and Outlay Account; the Sources and Uses of Funds, or Capital Reconciliation, or Resting Statement; and the Balance-sheet.

account which the foregoing considerations dictate must also hold to the fundamental distinction between fixed and variable, for it is implicit in the techniques of cost and management accountings that variable virtually means correlated. Sometimes I think that cost accounting has pushed this matter too far by limiting the variables to two main categories, cost of sales and sales, and by a temptation to tacitly assume that the one is necessarily correlated to the other in direct proportion. The standards of cost-accounting practice which are superposed in operating accounts tend to suggest an unwarranted attitude of certainty which they are far from possessing. They are much too absolute in the sense that by themselves they fail to prescribe upper and lower limits of tolerance. This is a trifle odd when we remember that they are usually nothing more than empirical estimates. It has always seemed to me that the real variances which ought to be studied by managements are those which move outside reasonably permissible limits.

11. There is a marked tendency amongst enthusiasts for management accounting to produce too many forms of account, and to make them available quite indiscriminately, presumably as a mark of efficiency, to *all* directors and other persons alike. In a large-scale organization there are many directors who are only concerned with issues which bear upon policy. They are not so much concerned with controllable expenditure as with having in front of them broad but frequent indicators to mark the trend of events both through the immediate past and into the immediate future. They are entitled to expect the administrative and management officers below them to control within reasonable limits those outgoings for which they are responsible. Detailed and frequent forms of account limited to the jurisdictions of each of these officers are plainly the source material for the exercise of this kind of control. But this material is not within the province of the main board unless its management officers are unreliable, in which case they should not be there at all. The main board requires simple, clear, and orderly forms which can be quickly assimilated and understood. Its members want to know about upward and downward trends in activity; whether or not they are peculiar to their own enterprise. Are there external factors causing disruption over the industry as a whole?

If so, how can they be countered? What are the expectations of the future and so on? Right policies depend upon right answers to these questions. It is still my view that at regular and periodical intervals each member of the board should be served with a clear but simple form of operating statement, appropriation account, balance-sheet, statement showing the source and use of funds,[1] and giving a plain indication of the disposal of depreciation provisions and saved income by real asset formation and changes in money claims, together with a short summary of proposed capital expenditure accompanied by its output and financial implications. When available the expectations for oncoming periods should be framed in similar forms. But this afternoon I want to concentrate on the form of operating account most suitable for this purpose, and I want to propose it in what I think are its fundamental categories, having regard to all that I have said before in this address. For the moment, however, I make my point that those management accounts which are prepared for the use of policy directors must be immediately clear and shorn of the intricacies of sheer mechanics. I never have been able to believe that a calendar variance has any real meaning for a policy director, for surely it is a permissible tolerance. Subsidiary information on the variances for material price and usage, labour efficiency and rates of pay, expense efficiencies, volume and expenditure, and calculations of activity and efficiency in terms of standard hours, should all be sent where they belong—to those responsible for detailed and sectional effectiveness.

12. I now turn to the operating account and I give it to you in the fundamental form set out on pages 78–79.

13. I do not think that any of you here will deny its simplicity, and I hope you will agree with me that it is appropriate to the requirements of policy directors. It is designed to show the limits of normal deviation from standards, and it should be accompanied by a concise report explaining the major causes of variance. It is essential that this explanatory document should be kept precise. You will notice that for the purposes of management the account is divided into two parts in order that it shall conform to the

[1] In my terminology, resting account.

OPERATING

Variable Inputs

	Actual	The expecta-tion	± Tolerance limits	Variance beyond tolerance
4. LABOUR—Wages and salaries and social insurance contributions				
(i) Direct or operative .	x	x	x	x
(ii) Ancillary . . .	x	x	x	x
(iii) Selling and distribution .	x	x	x	x
	x	x	x	x
5. VARIABLE MARGIN . .	x	x	x	x
	x	x	x	x
7. PURCHASES of goods and services related to operating facilities, and *not* directly varying with output. . . .	x	x	x	x
8. LABOUR—Wages, salaries, remuneration, and social insurance contributions allocated to Administration and management	x	x	x	x
9. CAPITAL				
(i) Rents (imputed or actual)				
(*a*) Factory . . .	x	x		
(*b*) Warehouse and sales-room . . .	x	x		
(*c*) Office . . .	x	x		
(ii) Depreciation of *real* assets	x	x	x	x
	x	x	x	x
10. OPERATING INCOME . .	x	x	x	x
	x	x	x	x

ACCOUNT

	Output			
	Actual	*The expecta-tion*	*± Tolerance limits*	*Variance beyond tolerance*
1. SALES of goods and services	x			
2. MINUS PURCHASES of goods and services . . .	x			
	x			
3. CHANGES in inventories .	x	x	x	x	x

x	x	x	x

6. VARIABLE MARGIN . .	x	x	x	x

x	x	x	x

See Appendix to my *Social Accounts and the Business Enterprise Sector of the National Economy* (Cambridge University Press, 1949) for the types of entries appearing under Purchases of goods and services.

cost-accounting notions of variable and fixed expense. I regard the right-hand side of the variable part as a matter of fundamental importance because it measures output, and I define output as the value added or created by the operating processes of production. It is also my view that the variable inputs are more likely than not to be correlated with output. If they are not correlated in a recognizable trend then I suggest something is amiss.

14. When this operating account is set to ends other than we are now considering, it does involve some problems of measurement which you will find discussed in a preliminary report of a sub-committee of the Research Committee on the subject of the measurement of productive efficiency.[1] This report also drew attention to the following types of efficiency ratios, which I should regard as useful accompaniments to the operating account.

1. Value of output per £ of operative labour cost.
2. Value of output per £ of real capital investment.
3. Value of output per head of operative labour.
4. Value of output per horse-power of plant utilization.
5. Operating income as a function of real capital investment.
6. Operating income as a function of output.
7. Operating income per unit of output.
8. Operating income as a function of the total input factor costs.

I think you should mark the significance of output as I have defined it, and portrayed it in the right-hand side of the variable part of the account, as a term in the majority of these relationships.

15. This concept of output is far reaching. Entrepreneurs tend to base their expectation of output on their experience of the past, and it is this expectation of output which tends to influence the rate of real capital investment and with it the capital inputs in the operating account. I know that in addition to this influence account must be taken of enterprise saving and its borrowing potentiality. In times of prosperity output tends to be overestimated and, vice versa, underestimated when things are bad. Existing accounting conventions assist in magnifying these changes in expectations. In good times, therefore, there is an inclination to over-increase or

[1] Published in *Accounting Research*, vol. ii, No. 2, Apr. 1951. See Appendix to this book.

exaggerate output capacity which may sow the seeds of its own downfall. The provoking possibility of surplus capacity should always be avoided.

From what I have said you will see that great care is necessary in setting standard outputs, and that every possible caution should be exercised to avoid over optimism and undue pessimism alike. Moreover, extreme care should be taken to see that plant extensions are *not* based on exaggerated output expectations.

16. The design of the operating account which I have set before you emphasizes the distinction between variable and fixed costs. I associate marginal costs with variable costs. The ultimate aim of this divided aggregate form of account is to assist the management in watching the progress of the enterprise towards a state in which effective minimum marginal costs and minimum effective fixed costs prevail. These are both essential to the maximization of operating income.

17. In the latter part of this paper I have sought to be practical and down to earth, by suggesting one or two fundamental simplicities of accounting form when this is ordered to the requirements of those at the top level of industrial management. But since you are at Oxford, even at Balliol, you will, I know, accept from me one last quotation on a rather different plane. Thus Maritain says it was: 'Aristotle who showed that an ontology of the sensible world is possible, not so far as it is sensible, but in so far as it is the world of *changing being*, and that it implies in its structure intelligible invariants dependent on specifying forms.'[1] The more I read philosophy the more I find in it so many of the fundamental answers to those practical problems which present themselves to applied techniques like our own. And there I must end this discussion of accounting form, leaving you to make of it what you will.

[1] *The Degrees of Knowledge*, by Jacques Maritain, p. 214 (Geoffrey Bles: The Centenary Press, 1937).

APPENDIX

THE MEASUREMENT OF PRODUCTIVE EFFICIENCY

PRELIMINARY REPORT

1. In the summer of 1950 a sub-committee of the Incorporated Accountants' Research Committee was constituted to investigate the accounting contribution to the measurement of productive efficiency. The opening discussions brought an understanding of the investigation in terms of the following aims:

    i. A disinterested and comprehensive review of the ideas so far put forward in the United Kingdom and other countries on the twin subjects of productivity measurement, and the measurement of productive efficiency.

    ii. The detection of simple pointers to changes in inputs correlated with changes in outputs, drawn from such accounts as can be designed for this purpose.

    iii. To promote and lend encouragement to a practical means of testing such answers as may be discovered from the pursuit of our second aim.

2. As Mr. L. H. Tippett has remarked,[1] 'perhaps the most important recent investigation suggesting the possibility of much increased productivity in British industry is that of Dr. L. Rostas who used data from the Census of Production and related sources to compare PMH (production per man-hour) in a number of manufacturing industries in the United Kingdom and the United States of America'. Dr. Rostas was kind enough to attend a meeting of the sub-committee, and explain his experience in this type of inquiry.

3. The sub-committee has received a mass of pertinent literature from many and diverse sources, all of which its members gladly acknowledge. It is obvious that there is no lack of ideas in this field, and the Research Committee of the Society of Incorporated Accountants hope that both published and unpublished material evidencing new developments will continue to be placed at the disposal of its sub-committee.

4. It cannot be denied that 'a nation's standard of living and competitive advantage in world trade depend upon continual improvement

[1] 'The Essentials for Increased Productivity', *The Three Banks Review*, Dec. 1950.

in productivity levels',[1] and much energy has been expended in devising a means of measurement which relates labour effort to product output. As one member of the sub-committee has put it, the first real impetus to the measurement of productivity came from the United States. It was a country with a wealth of natural resources and in the early days there were many people who wanted to be in business on their own account. Business expansion depended upon the ability to command labour. In such circumstances labour was scarce and valuable, and the best hope of expansion lay in the achievement of a greater output from the limited labour available. Accordingly every new project was looked upon in the light of labour saved and the common yardstick employed was the relationship of physical output to the number of workers employed, or to the number of man-hours utilized. Thus we are reminded that the value of the man-hour concept of productivity so devised depended very largely on the degree of scarcity of labour.

The same member of the sub-committee has pointed out that, in cases where the unit of output is easily recognizable and is constant in design and quality, an index expressed in terms of output per man-hour can give a valuable indication of the productivity of *labour*. If the labour force is reduced by mechanization the 'productivity' figure will increase, even though there may be increased expenses which more than offset the saving in labour. If the output consists of more than one type it may be necessary to weight the various types and the index will suffer because of the necessary approximation. These objections apply to all similar indexes which are based on physical measures of output.

From yet another source we see that 'the physical quantity of production attained by a given number of man-hours worked (or conversely, the number of man-hours required per unit of physical output) depends on a large number of separate, though interrelated, influences. The type of production methods in use, the age and condition of machinery, changes in product design, changes in work methods, and the relative degree of capacity utilization, all affect efficiency. In addition, the availability of parts and components, the efficiency of the managerial and labour forces, and industrial relations directly affect output per man-hour. It is usually impossible to isolate and measure the effect of any one of these without a detailed and costly engineering study.'[2] It hardly seems that these are problems capable of simple and immediate accounting solution.

[1] Serial No. R.1996, from the *Monthly Labor Review* (February 1950)—U.S. Labor Department's Bureau of Labor Statistics, IX—Measurement of Unit Man-Hour Requirements. [2] Serial No. R.1996. Op. cit.

Again, in a paper on *Technological Change and Productivity*, Mr. W. D. Evans, Chief of the Office of Labor Economics in the United States, remarks that: 'In seeking the sources of our increased productivity levels, it seems to have been fashionable to attribute them to labor, capital, or management. Actually, of course, the real foundation has been the steady accumulation of technical knowledge and its application to the jobs we wish to have done.' From such opinions as we have so far chosen to cite it is clear that productivity is not wholly dependent upon labour. Thus a measurement which relates productivity to man-hours can have but limited uses.

5. We may and should view our problem on a wide scale, and notice that some of the implications discussed at (4) claimed the support of Professor G. C. Allen in his presidential address before Section F of the British Association at Birmingham in September of last year. There and then he made it clear that our hopes for the future depend upon two factors, 'first, the continuance of those improvements in industrial technique and organisation which have been the chief proximate cause of economic progress so far, and, second, the preservation of full employment for a long time ahead'. Moreover, he was particularly mindful of the fact that 'high productivity is often the result of the way in which the capital resources are used, and is not determined solely by the quantity of them. The key, in other words, is to be found in organization.' Thus it is only a plain observation that 'fertility in resource and imaginative enterprise' lie at the root of productivity. 'I suggest, therefore, that the capitalisation of industry is a function of enterprise, and that the higher productivity which the extensive use of capital makes possible, depends ultimately on the supply of entrepreneurs.' Yet again, 'the rise in material wealth depends not so much upon steady progress in turning out familiar things (although of course that is important enough) as upon the discovery of new ways of producing those things and upon finding new things to produce'.

Accounting cannot take the place of fertility in resource and imaginative enterprise, but it can put safeguards on and measure the consequence of policies thus far designed and put into execution. As such it checks back-sliding and helps entrepreneurs to achieve a 'capacity for imposing their authority on their organisation and of persuading others to entrust them with the resources necessary for new ventures'.[1]

6. Conventional accounting measurements are expressed in monetary

---

[1] The quotations in para. 5 are taken from the print of Professor Allen's address in the *Economic Journal* for Sept. 1950.

terms. The measurement of productive effectiveness requires efforts to
be brought into correspondence with accomplishments, or, if we prefer more sophisticated language, inputs with outputs. If we isolate a
particular piece of economic activity, and compare over time the total
effort in resources utilized to achieve the total product output realized
by that operation, both measured in monetary terms and expressed as a
difference, then we have the common form of profit and loss account
familiar to accounting technique. We can also express total input as a
function of total output. Similarly, we can analyse total input in terms
of the contributing factors of production, and express each as a function
of total output, but it is unwise to rely on any one particular function if
the factor concerned is not significant when related to total input.

7. It is unnecessary to remind entrepreneurs, charged with the duty
of achieving a balanced use of productive resources, that some form of
accounts is an essential guide to the intelligent conduct of any business
enterprise. Latter-day accounting has become less directly concerned
with matters of accountability and stewardship, though it must always
preserve these functions, and more employed in setting bases for the
execution of successful policies. As is well known, such policies are
intimately associated with high levels of productivity, but although well
formulated accounts make for intelligent appreciation, they cannot take
the place of creative ability and wise judgement, both of which are
qualities to be looked for in the personal characters of the policy-makers.

8. The changed perspective of accounting to which we have referred
looks upon *productive efficiency* as best expressed in the relation between
output actually produced and that which should have been produced.
The measurement of this relationship requires the ascertainment of some
homogeneous unit with which to measure production and some standard
basis for calculating what should have been produced. Some accountants
contend that this is a simple matter when applied to a single operation
or a continuous process, and that reasonable comparisons can be made
between like processes or between the results of the same process in
different periods. They are careful to point out that although the method
is simple there is always the problem to be encountered of whether what
is measured is the efficiency of the operator or the efficiency of the stand-
ard-setter. Any attempt to make comparisons between the efficiency of
one firm and another, or even between one department and another, is
fraught with difficulties, the chief of which is the absence of uniformity
in setting standards. If we only look at this problem in a very general
sense it is easy to see that standards designed to indicate the best use of

such resources as a firm chances to have available may still be out of line with standards (admittedly ideally conceived) to indicate the best use of all possible resources open to that firm.

9. It has been put to us that the measurement of productive efficiency as applied to a single operation or process can be calculated on a simple time basis, and we are indebted to one of the members of our sub-committee for the following explanation.

'1. For every operation or process there needs to be fixed a standard output per hour, e.g. so many physical units to be produced in an hour. The total units produced divided by the standard hourly output gives the number of standard hours produced.

'2. For each operation there should be recorded:

(a) the total hours available,

(b) the total hours the machine or cost centre is actually working, and

(c) the standard hours produced.

'3. From these figures:

$$\frac{b \times 100}{a} \text{ is the figure of capacity usage,}$$

$$\frac{c \times 100}{b} \text{ is operating efficiency, and}$$

$\frac{c \times 100}{a}$ is a combination of the previous two factors, which may be described as "overall efficiency".'

Thus it is asserted that 'if every factory had these figures regularly for each operation or process, and an analysis of the difference between figure (a) and figure (b), it would have all the information necessary for making periodic comparisons of productivity and productive efficiency'. There can be little doubt that for the individual enterprise this approach has much to commend it.

10. Again, it has been remarked that operating efficiency can be increased by increasing costs. Thus it is highly desirable to see that any saving ascribed to increased efficiency is not outweighed by the increasing costs. The suggestion is advanced that this can be done by dividing the total costs of a particular period by the number of standard hours of work produced to arrive at the *actual* cost of a *standard* hour's work. The fluctuation of this hourly cost will give a measure of productive efficiency which takes into account both time and expenditure. It will

be seen that if a standard hourly cost has been computed as representing normal effectiveness then

$$\frac{\text{Standard cost of standard hour} \times 100}{\text{Actual cost of standard hour}} = \begin{array}{l}\text{Percentage productive effi-}\\ \text{ciency}\end{array}$$

This is equivalent to $\dfrac{\text{Standard cost}}{\text{Actual cost}} \times 100$, and may be calculated for any cost centre, department, or the factory as a whole. There is a drawback to this method of calculation, because there *are* items which can have an influence on costs, but which are not specifically related to the problem of operating efficiency, more particularly in the short period.

We add the comment that, before these methods are used for comparing one business with another, it is essential to ensure that standards are set on a comparable basis, that the same elements of cost are included in each comparison, and that standing charges are allocated in like manner. These are formidable prerequisites.

11. We have been invited by one of the members of our sub-committee to consider the measurement of productive efficiency in relation to the calculation of incentive payments, and in due time we may hope to give this problem our consideration. For the moment, however, we feel that our efforts should be concentrated on the accounting portrayal of productivity problems. It has also been proposed, from the same source, that our first excursion into the applied field should be limited to an industry with a product which is simple and easily measured. It is suggested that the impact of expanding capital on productivity might be more readily discernible in this situation. We recognize the possibility that some universal principles may be detectable where the productive processes are simple and the output is homogeneous, and we may start on this basis when the opportunity presents itself.

12. In so far as an account is brought to the service of productivity measurement it must relate outputs to inputs, both expressed in monetary terms. We have noticed that operative labour is not the only relevant input, for some regard must be paid to management, and the employment of *real* operating assets unconfused by the presence of monetary claims in assessments of capital employed. But there are problems. Increases in productivity can be passed on to both consumers and employees. Consumers may benefit either by lower prices or by better-quality products or services. The form of an account can be manipulated to reveal the former, but less readily and far less simply, the latter. Employees may benefit either by increased wages or by happier working

conditions and such-like advantages. The former may be directly expressed in an account while the latter may be indirectly concealed. Nevertheless, it must be our aim to evolve a form of account which will record details appropriate to a general interpretive measurement of changes in output for given inputs, and the expression of a production function based upon a monetary assessment of real product.

13. It should be commented that occasionally information taken from accounts, as conventionally drawn, has been utilized for simple productivity investigations. The principal item usually relied upon is *gross* output. This is expressed in terms of per £100 of operative labour and per £100 of capital employed. These are types of ratios favoured in farm and grassland investigations.[1] Further refinements introduced into these latter types of investigation yield ratios which depend upon the division of gross output into cash crops and livestock. Both classifications of gross output are expressed in terms of acreage, adjusted for land fertilities, so that the ratio is calculated as gross output per adjusted acre. Again, gross livestock output can be expressed in terms of per £100 of feeding-stuffs. These types of accounting ratios can and often do point to general trends when related to an array of entities, displaying similar qualities and fulfilling similar functions, and where the aim is inter-entity comparison; but there is plainly a weakness in a capital measure which relies upon balance-sheets, as conventionally drawn, with real assets basically valued from the standpoint of historical cost.

14. Some of us are attracted to the concept of value added by the organization and utilization of production factors in operating activity. For one thing it is susceptible to accounting treatment. Purchases of goods and services, adjusted for changes in inventories (a device for carrying over unmatched costs from one accounting period to another), when brought within the net of the operating activity of a period of account, are transformed into sales of goods and services at the values placed upon them in the market. We therefore subscribe to the following view expressed in Bulletin 913 of the United States Department of Labor: 'Granted that there are elements of monopoly and of Government price fixing, the value added figures reflect, as nearly as anything, the combined judgments of the community.'[2] There are two other comments in this Bulletin which have claimed our accounting attention.

---

[1] Cf. 'Farm Costing and Grassland Investigation', *An Economic and Financial Analysis*, 1948, by G. H. N. Pettit (Imperial Chemical Industries Ltd. C.A.C. Development Department, Apr. 1950).

[2] Op. cit., p. 40.

The first, that it should be possible 'to develop a series of ratios, relating output to the various categories of labor and not merely to labor input as a whole. Changes in the proportion of overhead workers may not be only a cyclical relationship; it has been suggested that there is a decided trend in this country (America) toward an increase in the proportion of overhead workers.'[1] The second offers the very interesting interpretive proposal that 'if a series of ratios is prepared, with the various inputs in the numerators and the output in the denominator, one might say that the relationship which changed least from one year to the next was probably the factor which most nearly accounted for the change in production'.[2] We now begin to sense some of the formal properties of a productivity account.

15. There is one major problem which has to be faced in giving accounting significance to the 'value added' concept. We refer to the possible presence of windfall gains and losses which bear no direct relation to operating activity. These are usually the outcome of marked changes in those prices which directly affect the purchases or sales of goods and services entering into the calculation of the product of activity. They tend to promote windfall profits or losses which are (temporarily at least) unrelated to the factor costs of activity. In so far as is possible the influence of these changes should be removed from the operating account to be separately dealt with in the appropriation account.

16. The concept of 'value added' suggests to us other variations in the accounting treatment of its make-up. Thus we are inclined to the view that where there has been significant inventory formation on account of work in progress or process, and finished goods, then it is better that this change should be lifted from its conventional valuation in terms of cost to a valuation in terms of market selling prices. The intention of this variation is to secure the homogeneous measurement of output. Again, we think that a significant change in the opening and closing inventories of raw materials, which have been the subject of price change within the currency of the period of account, is better valued at last cost rather than first cost.

17. To recapitulate the accounting implications of productivity measurement, we hold the view that an operating account designed in 'value added' (product) terms can be formulated for any piece of economic activity, whether it be a process, a plant, a department, or indeed the productive entity itself. Measures of productivity may then be sought in financial and related physical terms. As we have previously hinted, some

---

[1] Ibid., p. 15.   [2] Ibid., p. 48.

of the more common expressions of these measures are similar to those set out below:

Value of product per £ of operative labour cost.

Value of product per £ of real capital investment (valued in terms of current costs).

Value of product per head of operative labour.

Value of product per horse-power of plant utilization.

Operating surplus or profit is itself a test of effectiveness (whatever may be said to the contrary), since it measures the difference between the value added by reason of the activity and the total inputs so engaged. Efficiency ratios using operating surplus suggest themselves in the following terms:

Operating surplus as a function of the current value of the *real* assets employed in the activity.

Operating surplus per unit of output.

Operating surplus as a function of the total input factor costs.

Operating surplus as a function of the product.

We take the view that measures of productivity and productive efficiency other than those dwelt on at one point or another in this report may show themselves when the operating account in terms of value added is brought into use in the applied field. Quite plainly, however, more than one measure will be required to achieve anything like a reasonable understanding of the changes which may arise when one accounting period is compared with another, and when one unit of activity is brought into contrast with another.

18. We set out on the opposite page a suggested simple form of operating account designed to meet the accounting implications of our inquiry.

19. We desire to emphasize our awareness that one of the most fundamental problems of productivity accounting has only been partially touched upon in this preliminary report. We refer to the difficult question of valuing inputs and outputs at constant prices. Clearly, if this *is* achieved, we can establish a ratio of total factor inputs to product which will measure changes in *real* productivity. We are hoping to give time to a careful investigation of this subject, and we expect to deal with it in a later report. For the present it must suffice to indicate that the lines on which we are working bear a resemblance to the application of those predetermined cost and value rates which are so familiar a feature of present-day cost accounting technique. We envisage a schedule giving

OPERATING ACTIVITY

Input allocations				*Output value added*	
I. LABOUR—Wages and salaries and social insurance contributions				I. NET SALES of goods and services* . .	x
(i) Direct or operative . . .	x			II. MINUS net purchases of goods and services† varying with output .	x
(ii) Ancillary . .	x	x			x
(iii) Selling and distribution . .		x		III. CHANGES in inventories‡	x
(iv) Administration and management		x	x	IV. MINUS net purchases of goods and services related to productive facilities, *not* varying with output . .	x
II. CAPITAL					
(i) Rents (imputed or actual)					
(1) Factory .	x				
(2) Warehouse and salesroom	x				
(3) Office . .	x	x			
(ii) Depreciation of *real* assets, measured in terms of end-period prices[1]	x				
(iii) Interest on *real* assets (excluding buildings), employed during the period of account, and measured in terms of end-period prices .	x	x			
		x			
III. OPERATING SURPLUS .		x			
		x		TOTAL VALUE ADDED .	x

NOTES:

* After deducting returns, allowances, discounts, and bad debts.

† After deducting returns, allowances, and discounts. Indirect taxes are included in purchases.

‡ Subject to the valuation suggestions made in the text.

outputs and inputs at actual and standard values. Output at standard value will be related to a £ of input at standard value, and the productivity change in output per £ of input calculated. Thereafter it should be a simple matter to construct a productivity index for any one piece of operating activity.

[1] We are aware that this conceptual measurement involves serious practical difficulties.

20. On the general question of the productive efficiency of the individual enterprise we should like to draw attention to the usefulness of such well-known subsidiary statistical information[1] as is represented by the following:

i. Details of unused resources, particularly space and plant.

ii. Activity accounts in which the expenses associated with outputs are limited to those which would be eliminated if the particular activity ceased.

iii. Stability of labour in terms of the *rate* of labour turnover.

iv. Output of service rendered expressed in terms of personnel employed.

v. Rates of turnover, e.g. gross output to inventories, or the total of *real* assets employed.

21. We are sensitive to the fact that the whole question of increased productivity is much wider and deeper than mere accounting indexes can reveal. We have only to instance the type of consideration which received careful comment in Sir Geoffrey Heyworth's speech at the annual general meeting of Lever Brothers and Unilever Ltd. in July 1950, and in Mr. L. H. Tippett's article on 'The Essentials for Increased Productivity' which appeared in *The Three Banks Review* for December 1950, to substantiate this. Nevertheless, we retain the conviction that the aims which we cited at the start of this report have point and are worth pursuing, and we shall welcome any ideas which can lend precision to the kind of solutions we are seeking.

22. The following members of the Society of Incorporated Accountants are serving on this sub-committee of the Research Committee:

Mr. W. B. Barrett
Mr. F. Sewell Bray
Mr. T. Haworth
Mr. C. E. Sutton

In addition Mr. H. Ingham of the British Institute of Management has shown a deep interest in our work. He has consistently attended our meetings, and has contributed memoranda for discussion. We are grateful for the time and effort which he is so readily placing at the disposal of the sub-committee.

[1] Cf. *The Monthly Statement as a Management Tool.* Written for the Industrial and Commercial Finance Corporation by David Solomons (1950).

PRINTED IN
GREAT BRITAIN
AT THE
UNIVERSITY PRESS
OXFORD
BY
CHARLES BATEY
PRINTER
TO THE
UNIVERSITY